The Hidden and Manifest God

SUNY Series in Judaica:
Hermeneutics, Mysticism, and Religion

Michael Fishbane, Robert Goldenberg, and Arthur Green, editors

The Hidden and Manifest God

Some Major Themes in Early Jewish Mysticism

Peter Schäfer

Translated by Aubrey Pomerance

STATE UNIVERSITY OF NEW YORK PRESS

Published by
State University of New York Press, Albany

Printed in the United States of America

For information, address State University of New York Press, State University Plaza, Albany, N.Y., 12246

Production by Dana Foote
Marketing by Theresa A. Swierzowski

Library of Congress Cataloging in Publication Data

Schäfer, Peter, 1943–
The hidden and manifest God : some major themes in early Jewish mysticism / Peter Schäfer.
p. cm.—(SUNY series in Judaica.)
Includes bibliographical references and index.
ISBN 0–7914–1043–9 (CH : acid-free).—ISBN 0–7914–1044–7 (PB : acid-free)
1. Mysticism—Judaism—History. 2. Heikhalot rabbati. 3. Heikhalot zutrati. 4. Merkava. 5. Shiʿur komah. 6. Hebrew book of Enoch. I. Title. II. Series.
BM526.S284 1992
296.1'6—dc20 *91-23058*
CIP

10 9 8 7 6 5 4 3 2 1

In memoriam

Arnold Goldberg
1928–1991

Contents

Preface

The following study lays open to discussion my view of the most important elements and aspects of early Jewish mysticism. After ten years of intensive work dealing above all with the literary side of Merkavah mysticism, I feel that the time has come to attempt to summarize its essential designs and goals, both against the background of rabbinic Judaism and in confrontation with it.

However, the present contribution, as is the case with all my studies, stems from the premise that the "message" of literature can only be grasped through a continual exploration of the texts, their literary form, and their development. The growing number of complaints now to be heard against the assumed predominance of a literary approach in studies on Hekhalot literature, as opposed to its interpretation as a mystical experience, are probably a trend of research; in the end, however, such a trend presents only a spurious alternative. The extraction of authentic mystical experience from Hekhalot literature remains but interpretation of this literature and likewise requires the examination of the literary forms and their redactional processes if it wishes to satisfy historical demands. One of the main reasons why research has distanced itself from Scholem's interpretation of Merkavah mysticism as a mysticism of experience is Scholem's general and much too bold disregard for the literary origin of this literature and its rules of form and development.

This study pursues considerations that I first published in 1986 under the title "Gershom Scholem Reconsidered: The Aim and Purpose of Early Jewish Mysticism" as the Twelfth Sacks Lecture of the Oxford Centre for Postgraduate Hebrew Studies (and also printed in my ***Hekhalot-Studien,*** Tübingen 1988). Parts of earlier versions were presented in November 1987 as the Franz Delitzsch Lecture at the University of Münster and in May 1990 as the Third Magie Lecture at the University of Princeton. The major part of the final version was written during two sojourns as a Visiting Fellow at Wolfson College of the University of Oxford. In view of the rapid progress of Hekhalot research it is self-evident that this present version as well can only be seen as an intermediate result. My colleagues and students at the Institut für Judaistik in Berlin have contributed much toward this progress. I am indebted to them for their critical review of my work, above all to Klaus Herrmann and Claudia Rohrbacher-Sticker. I wish to thank Hannelore Liss and Gottfried Reeg for providing the index. Further thanks are due to Aubrey Pomerance for translating the German manuscript into English and to Michael Fishbane for kindly reading the English version and contributing some important suggestions.

Shortly after I completed the German version of this manuscript, Arnold Goldberg, my teacher in Germany, passed away. For all of those close to him and his work, his death was premature. I owe much to his personal example, his sensitive conveyance of rabbinic thought, and his criticism. It is to his memory that the present study is dedicated, in reverence and in gratitude.

Berlin, November 1991

Peter Schäfer

1

Introduction

Those secret signatures (*Rischumim*), which God placed in things, are to be sure to the same degree concealments of his revelation as revelation of his concealment. . . . As such, the revelation is one of the name or names of God, which are perhaps the various modi of his active being. The language of God has namely no grammar. It consists only of names.

—Gershom Scholem,
"Tradition und Kommentar als
religiöse Kategorien im Judentum"

Of the various phases of Jewish mysticism, which up until now only Gershom Scholem has attempted to represent in their entirety,[1] the earliest has enjoyed increased attention by scholars of Jewish studies over the past several years.[2] It is the first "mystical"

---

[1]*Major Trends in Jewish Mysticism*, 3d ed., New York, 1954; London, 1955 [1941]; a new overall view is being prepared by Joseph Dan.

[2]Cf. G. Scholem, *Jewish Gnosticism, Merkabah Mysticism, and Talmudic Tradition*, 2d ed., New York, 1965 [1960]; J. Maier, *Vom Kultus zur Gnosis*, Salzburg, 1964;

movement tangible within a complete literary system in whose center stands the divine chariot as described by Ezekiel (chapters 1 and 10) and that thus has been termed *Merkavah mysticism.*[3] The type of literature in which we find this mysticism is called *Hekhalot literature;* that is, the literature that deals with the *hekhalot,* the heavenly "palaces" or "halls" through which the mystic passes to reach the divine throne. It is no coincidence that the term *hekhal* is taken from the architecture of the temple, where it is used precisely for the entrance hall to the holiest of holies. Whoever undertakes the dangerous ascent to the divine throne is called the *yored merkavah,* literally one who "descends" to the chariot.[4]

I. Gruenwald, *Apocalyptic and Merkavah Mysticism,* Leiden and Cologne, 1980 [AGAJU 14]; D. J. Halperin, *The Merkabah in Rabbinic Literature,* New Haven, Conn., 1980 [AOS 62]; P. Schäfer (ed.), *Synopse zur Hekhalot-Literatur,* Tübingen, 1981 [TSAJ 2]; I. Chernus, *Mysticism in Rabbinic Judaism,* Berlin and New York, 1982 [SJ 11]; M. S. Cohen, *The Shiʿur Qomah. Liturgy and Theurgy in Pre-Kabbalistic Jewish Mysticism,* Lanham, New York, and London, 1983; P. Schäfer (ed.), *Geniza-Fragmente zur Hekhalot-Literatur,* Tübingen, 1984 [TSAJ 6]; M. S. Cohen, *The Shiʿur Qomah: Texts and Recensions,* Tübingen 1985 [TSAJ 9]; P. S. Alexander, "Appendix: 3 Enoch," in E. Schürer, G. Vermes, F. Millar, and M. Goodman, *The History of the Jewish People in the Age of Jesus Christ,* vol. 3.1, Edinburgh, 1986, pp. 269ff.; idem, "Incantations and Books of Magic", in ibid., *The History of the Jewish People in the Age of Jesus Christ,* vol. 3.1, pp. 342ff.; P. Schäfer (ed.), *Konkordanz zur Hekhalot-Literatur,* vol. 1, Tübingen, 1986 [TSAJ 12], vol. 2, 1988 [TSAJ 13]; M. Bar-Ilan, *Sitre tefilla we-hekhalot,* Ramat-Gan, 1987; J. Dan (ed.), *Proceedings of the First International Conference on the History of Jewish Mysticism: Early Jewish Mysticism,* Jerusalem, 1987 [JSJT 6, 1–2]; P. Schäfer (ed.), *Übersetzung der Hekhalot-Literatur,* vol. 2: sections 81–334, Tübingen, 1987 [TSAJ 17]; I. Gruenwald, *From Apocalypticism to Gnosticism. Studies in Apocalypticism, Merkavah Mysticism and Gnosticism,* Frankfurt am Main, Bern, New York, and Paris 1988 [BEATAJ 14]; D. Halperin, *The Faces of the Chariot. Early Jewish Responses to Ezekiel's Vision,* Tübingen, 1988 [TSAJ 16]; P. Schäfer, *Hekhalot-Studien,* Tübingen 1988 [TSAJ 19]; P. Schäfer (ed.), *Übersetzung der Hekhalot-Literatur,* vol. 3: sections 335–597, Tübingen 1989 [TSAJ 22]; N. Janowitz, *The Poetics of Ascent. Theories of Language in a Rabbinic Ascent Text,* Albany, N.Y., 1989; P. Schäfer (ed.), *Übersetzung der Hekhalot-Literatur,* vol. 4: sections 598–985, Tübingen 1991 [TSAJ 29]; M. D. Swartz, "Liturgical Elements in Early Jewish Mysticism: A Literal Analysis of 'Maʿaseh Merkavah'," diss. New York University 1986.

[3]Although the term *merkavah* is not to be found in Ezekiel, but rather only *kisse,* "throne"; cf. Ezekiel 1:26, 10:1, 43:7. It is found in the technical sense, i.e. for the divine chariot in the temple (!), for the first time in 1 Chronicles 28:18. In Sirach 49:8 the *merkavah* (in Hebrew: *zene merkavah,* "types of the *merkavah*"; in Greek, *epi harmatos cheroubin,* "on the Cherub chariot") stands for the content of the Ezekiel vision; cf. also LXX Ezekiel 43:3.

[4]This paradoxical terminology, which uses the term *yarad* (literally, "descent") for the "ascent" to the Merkavah and the term *ʿalah* (literally, "ascent") for the "descent,"

I

It is a controversial point to what extent the movement or direction of Judaism, as expressed in the Hekhalot literature, can be defined as mysticism. In his magnum opus *Major Trends in Jewish Mysticism* (in the first chapter) Scholem discusses in detail the problems surrounding the definition of mysticism and Jewish mysticism. Among others, he refers to Rufus Jones's *Studies in Mystical Religion*[5] and Thomas Aquinas. Jones defines mysticism in the following way: "I shall use the word to express the type of religion which puts the emphasis on immediate awareness of relation with God, on direct and intimate consciousness of the Divine Presence. It is religion in its most acute, intense and living stage."[6] Scholem then consentingly quotes Thomas Aquinas's definition that mysticism is *cognitio dei experimentalis,* thus experimental knowledge of God obtained through living experience, whereby Thomas, like many mystics, refers to the words of the Psalm: "Oh taste and see that the Lord is good" (Psalms 34:9).[7] "It is this tasting and seeing," says Scholem, "however spiritualized it may become, that the genuine mystic desires" and he then submits his own definition: "His attitude is determined by the fundamental experience of the inner self which enters into immediate contact with God or the metaphysical Reality.

has not yet been conclusively explained; cf. Scholem, *Major Trends in Jewish Mysticism,* pp. 46f.; *Jewish Gnosticism,* p. 20, n. 1. The Hekhalot literature is, however, not consistent: the "reversed" use of *yarad* and *'alah* appears to be characteristic above all of *Hekhalot Rabbati;* against this, the other macroforms associate in the semantically "correct" way *'alah* with "ascent" and *yarad* with "descent." Whereby Scholem attempted to explain the paradoxical use of *yarad* through the analogy of the descent to the Torah shrine (*yored lifne ha-tevah*) in the synagogue service (*Jewish Gnosticism,* p. 20, n. 1) and later took refuge in a psychological explanation ("perhaps it means those who reach down into themselves in order to perceive the chariot?": Art. Kabbalah, *EJ* 10, Jerusalem 1971, col. 494), Halperin has recently referred to the parallels that speak of the descent of the Israelites to the Red Sea (*The Faces of the Chariot,* pp. 226ff.): "These writers had learned from midrashic traditions like the one preserved in *Ex.R.* 23:14 that the *merkabah* had been perceptible *in* the waters of the Red Sea when the Israelites crossed it. They deduced that access to what is above lies through what is below. To get up to the *merkabah,* one must descend" (p. 237). The one explanation remains as unsatisfactory as the other. See now E. Wolfson, "Descent to the Throne: Enthronement and Ecstasy in Ancient Jewish Mysticism," to appear in B. Herrera (ed.), *Typologies of Mysticism.*

[5]London, 1909.

[6]Quoted by Scholem, *Major Trends in Jewish Mysticism,* p. 4.

[7]*Summa theologiae* II-II, q. 97, a. 2.

What forms the essence of this experience, and how it is to be adequately described—that is the great riddle which the mystics themselves, no less than the historians, have tried to solve."[8]

Thus for Scholem, the essence of both mysticism and Jewish mysticism is made up of "the immediate contact with God" gained from the "fundamental experience of the inner self." The general history of religion has employed the expression *unio mystica* for this fundamental experience, the mystical unification with God. Scholem is very careful in assessing whether and to what extent this term is also applicable to Jewish mysticism. If it implies the coalescence of human existence with that of the divine being, the extinguishing of the mystics' individuality (in later Hasidic terminology *biṭṭul ha-yesh,* the "annihilation of the self"), then according to Scholem this applies only to a few manifestations of Jewish mysticism. For Scholem, the *unio mystica* is apparently the highest stage of mystical experience; other stages, which are more often to be found in Jewish mysticism, are ecstasy and, obviously under the influence of Gnosticism, that which Scholem calls the *soaring of the soul.* This experience, he argues, is particularly characteristic of early Jewish mysticism: "The earliest Jewish mystics who formed an organized fraternity in Talmudic times and later, describe their experience in terms derived from the diction characteristic of their age. They speak of the ascent of the soul to the Celestial Throne where it obtains an ecstatic view of the majesty of God and the secrets of His Realm."[9]

Scholem introduced two further terms to explain and illustrate the notion of "Jewish mysticism": *theosophy* and *esoteric. Theosophy* ("the wisdom of God") describes an aspect with regard to the contents of Jewish mysticism; namely, that it is concerned with exploring the mysteries of the hidden divine life and the relationship between the divine life and the world of human kind and creation. Insofar as this relationship is a reciprocal one, not only the world of God influencing the human world but human kind also influencing the divine inner life, one speaks of theurgy (*theourgia:* in the furthest sense from "divine action," which flows from both God and human beings, to "the coercion of God," the direct influence of human kind upon God with a strong magical component).

---

[8]*Major Trends in Jewish Mysticism,* p. 4.
[9]Ibid., p. 5.

Finally, the term *esoteric* pertains to the social side of the mystic: the "initiate," who is in possession of mystical knowledge, is forbidden to transmit it further; the circle of initiates is thus intentionally and artificially circumscribed. The secret knowledge is not for everyone, it requires particular ethical qualities, a specific age or also a limited number of adepts. It is already stipulated in the Mishnah that the central content of the secret teaching, in rabbinic terminology *ma*ʿ*aseh merkavah* ("working of the chariot") and *ma*ʿ*aseh bereshit* ("working of creation"), is subject to certain restrictions: "One does not expound cases of incest before three persons, the work of creation before two, and the Merkavah before one, unless he is wise and understands on his own."[10]

Due to simplicity, I have followed the convention set by Scholem and retained the term *mysticism,* even though its strong individualistic leaning limits the concerns of the Hekhalot literature to one aspect only.[11] The circles that formed this literature were engaged in nothing less than a radical transformation of the conception of the world of the so-called classical or normative Judaism,[12] which for centuries was determined by the rabbis; and this transformation, which in reality equals a revolution, is inadequately understood by the term *mysticism.*

II

The textual basis for a portrayal of early Jewish mysticism is the so-called Hekhalot literature. The editions of the *Synopse* and the *Geniza-Fragmente,* as well as the *Übersetzung,* have indeed made the most important text material of the Hekhalot literature accessible;

---

[10]M Ḥag 2:1.

[11]Gruenwald (*From Apocalypticism to Gnosticism,* p. 185) wishes to let the term *mysticism* in the Hekhalot literature stand only for the heavenly journey, but not for the theurgic-magical *sar ha-torah* traditions. This thesis not only presumes a much more rigid separation between the two central themes of the Hekhalot literature than is suggested by the literature itself (see below pp. 137ff.), but it also stems from a notion of religious-mystical experience that is not as self-evident as Gruenwald believes: "Mystical experiences, or for that matter visions of heavenly ascents . . . , are by all means the climax of one's religious life. All other religious experiences fall short of that, including for that matter the technique and experiences which come under the cover of the Sar-Torah complex of traditions" (ibid., p. 188).

[12]With this, however, the question is by no means decided whether this process took place *during* the heydey of rabbinic Judaism (i.e., simultaneously) or thereafter; see below pp. 159f.

however, the next essential step, the critical analysis of the literary, redactional, and traditional aspects is still in its infancy. The most significant result of investigations undertaken so far[13] has been to show that we are dealing with an extremely fluctuating literature that has been crystallized in various macroforms,[14] which are nonetheless interwoven with one another on many different levels. As has been illustrated by the Genizah fragments in particular, the redactional arrangement of the microforms into clearly defined "works" is to be placed rather at the end of the process than at the beginning (although the individual texts must be judged differently and opposite tendencies will likely also appear).[15] Even more differentiated and complicated is the picture when one compares individual sets of traditions and smaller literary units on the level of "microforms" with one another, which can appear in various relationships within the various macroforms.[16]

---

[13] Cf. above all *Hekhalot-Studien* and the cited literature.

[14] I employ the term *macroform* for a superimposed literary unit, instead of the terms *writing* or *work*, to accommodate the fluctuating character of the texts of the Hekhalot literature. The term *macroform* concretely denotes both the fictional or imaginary single text, which we initially and by way of delimitation always refer to in scholarly literature (e.g., *Hekhalot Rabbati* in contrast to *Maʿaseh Merkavah*, etc.), as well as the often different manifestations of this text in the various manuscripts. The border between micro- and macroforms is thereby fluent: certain definable textual units can be both part of a superimposed entirety (and thus a "microform") as well as an independently transmitted redactional unit (thus a "macroform"). An example of this would be the *sar ha-torah* unit, which is transmitted both as a part of *Hekhalot Rabbati* and as an independent "writing." Cf. in detail *Hekhalot-Studien*, pp. 199ff.

[15] The considerable differences between the Genizah fragments and the comprehensive medieval manuscripts, which lie not so much in the text variations but above all in the structure of the particular texts, have given rise to the assumption that we are dealing with two very different recensions of the Hekhalot literature; namely, an early "eastern" or "oriental" recension, which is represented by the Genizah fragments (which themselves are anything but uniform, but rather extremely varied and manifold), and a later "Ashkenazi" recension, which attempted to unify the transmitted material of the traditions. Cf. J. Dan, "Hekhalot genuzim", *Tarbiz* 56 (1987): 433–437; Schäfer, *Hekhalot-Studien*, pp. 3ff.

[16] Cf. (for *Hekhalot Rabbati*) *Hekhalot-Studien*, pp. 214f. It is a gross and distorted misunderstanding when Gruenwald argues against my "literary approach": "If the major concern of the scholar who studies that literature is restricted to structural problems as dictated by the rather fragmentary and flexible condition of the material as it appears in the manuscripts, then the intellectual interest one takes in the activities of the Merkavah mystics recedes to the background and is likely even to be buried in textual problems" (*From Apocalypticism to Gnosticism*, p. 180). Such a simplified contrast of "mere textual criticism" and "intellectual interest" really no longer should

The macroforms that undisputedly belong to the Hekhalot literature are *Hekhalot Rabbati* ("the Greater Palaces"), *Hekhalot Zuṭarti* ("the Lesser Palaces"), *Maʿaseh Merkavah* ("the Working of the Chariot), *Merkavah Rabbah* ("the Great Chariot"), and the so-called third book of Enoch (i.e., the Hebrew as opposed to the Ethiopian and Slavic books of Enoch); the macroforms whose affiliation is problematic above all are *Re'uyyot Yehezqel* ("the Visions of Ezekiel") and *Masekhet Hekhalot* ("the Tractate of the Hekhalot").[17] With the exception of *Re'uyyot Yehezqel*[18] and *Masekhet Hekhalot,*[19] the macroforms are edited in the *Synopse;* this edition, together with the edition of the Genizah fragments[20] and the respective volumes of translation,[21] is the basis for the following study.

With regard to dating the individual macroforms, scholarship is still far from reaching a consensus; this is valid for both an absolute and a relative chronology. As to the absolute chronology, Scholem's decisively held theory[22] that Merkavah mysticism stands in the center of rabbinic Judaism and reaches into the first and

---

be discussed. It is not a matter of textual criticism as an end in itself, but rather one of "contextual conclusions" that accommodate the textual and above all redactional particularities of the macroforms. How complicated these really are and how much remains to be done in this area is illustrated by the excellent contribution by K. Herrmann and C. Rohrbacher-Sticker, "Magische Traditionen der New Yorker Hekhalot-Handschrift JTS 8128 im Kontext ihrer Gesamtredaktion," *FJB* 17 (1989) 101–149. My own attempt in the present study will fulfill this demand only to a certain degree; see below pp. 8f. and 156f. with n. 35.

[17]On the question of the delimitation of the Hekhalot literature in general, see *Überstezung der Hekhalot-Literature,* vol. 2, pp. viiff.; *Hekhalot-Studien,* pp. 8ff. Concerning the size, delimitation, and structure of the macroforms, see *Hekhalot-Studien,* pp. 63ff., 201ff.; *Übersetzung der Hekhalot-Literatur,* vol. 2, pp. xivff. (*Hekhalot Rabbati*); *Hekhalot-Studien,* pp. 50ff.; *Übersetzung der Hekhalot-Literatur,* vol. 3, pp. viiff. (*Hekhalot Zuṭarti*); *Hekhalot-Studien,* pp. 218ff.; *Übersetzung der Hekhalot-Literatur,* vol. 3, pp. xxviiff. (*Maʿaseh Merkavah*); *Hekhalot-Studien,* pp. 17ff. (*Merkavah Rabbah*); *Hekhalot-Studien,* pp. 84ff.; 221ff. (3 Enoch).

[18]See the edition by I. Gruenwald, in *Temirin,* vol. 1, Jerusalem, 1972, pp. 101–139; S. A. Wertheimer, *Batei Midrashot,* 2d ed., vol. 2, Jerusalem, 1954, pp. 127–34.

[19]An edition with translation and commentary has been prepared by K. Herrmann.

[20]See above, p. 1, n. 2.

[21]Ibid.

[22]Against the older research by L. Zunz (*Die gottesdienstlichen Vorträge der Juden historisch entwickelt,* Berlin 1832 [2d ed., Frankfurt am Main, 1892], pp. 165ff.) and above all by H. Graetz ("Die mystische Literatur in der gaonäischen Epoche," *MGWJ* 8 [1859] 67–78, 103–118, 140–153), who postulated an origin in the ninth century and under the influence of Islam.

second centuries C.E. has determined scholarship up until the present time.[23] Only recently have voices been heard that argue for a later dating[24] and view an absolute dating of the Hekhalot literature in general as being of little help. This is due mostly to the complicated redactional process and the widely differing literary levels within the macroforms, and further, to their fluctuating borders.[25] On the question of the relative chronology, Scholem inaugurated the sequence *Reʾuyyot Yehezqel, Hekhalot Zuṭarti, Hekhalot Rabbati, Merkavah Rabbah, Maʿaseh Merkavah,* 3 Enoch, and *Masekhet Hekhalot,* more intuitively than based on solid evidence (although he often emphasized the particularly old age of *Hekhalot Zuṭarti*).[26] This sequence, for the most part, has been adopted by scholars.[27] The following study diverts from this convention and adopts the sequence *Hekhalot Rabbati, Hekhalot Zuṭarti, Maʿaseh Merkavah, Merkavah Rabbah,* and 3 Enoch, which is supported by several observations in the analyzed texts.[28]

III

The deciphering of the literary, redactional, and traditional-historical relations of the Hekhalot literature is an important prerequisite for any intensive study of its contents. The following attempt to understand some of the main claims of the Hekhalot literature is undertaken in the full realization of the temporariness of this venture. Insofar as the analysis will limit itself to the macroforms *Hekhalot Rabbati, Hekhalot Zuṭarti, Maʿaseh Merkavah, Merkavah Rabbah,* and 3 Enoch in their more or less accepted range, not only will certain macroforms remain disregarded, but so will insertions

---

[23]*Major Trends in Jewish Mysticism,* p. 45; *Jewish Gnosticism,* p. 24; idem, *Origins of the Kabbalah,* Princeton, N.J., 1987, p. 19. Cf. *Übersetzung der Hekhalot-Literatur,* vol. 2, pp. xxff.

[24]Halperin, *The Merkabah in Rabbinic Literature,* pp. 3ff., 183ff.; idem, *The Faces of the Chariot,* pp. 360ff.

[25]Schäfer, *Hekhalot-Studien,* pp. 8ff.; *Übersetzung der Hekhalot-Literatur,* vol. 2, pp. xxff.; vol. 3, pp. xvif., xxxiiff.; Swartz, *Liturgical Elements,* pp. 276ff.

[26]Cf. for example, *Major Trends in Jewish Mysticism,* p. 45; *Jewish Gnosticism,* p. 76; see also below, p. 151, n. 13.

[27]Gruenwald, *Apocalyptic and Merkavah Mysticism,* pp. 134ff., follows this order exactly; cf. also Schäfer, *Hekhalot-Studien,* pp. 8ff.

[28]See below, p. 156, n. 35. *Reʾuyyot Yehezqel* and *Masekhet Hekhalot* are not taken into account because they are not considered to belong to the Hekhalot literature proper.

and sets of traditions on the peripheries of the macroforms, whose affiliation is difficult to ascertain, be neglected. The basis of the text, therefore, is of necessity limited and—for want of adequate preliminary examinations—to a certain degree also artificial. Nonetheless, an attempt will be made, as far as possible, to explore the affiliations of the macroforms and especially the literary layers within the macroforms to present a more complex representation.

As stated, the theme that Scholem saw as central in the Hekhalot literature is the "heavenly journey of the soul," the ascent of the Merkavah mystic through the seven heavenly palaces to the divine throne. This theme undoubtedly is an important motif whose significance, however, (under the influence of the gnostic literature) is presumed rather than proven by a comprehensive analysis. As shall be illustrated, this premise has led to a rather distorted overall evaluation of the Hekhalot literature. Therefore, the following study will be guided not so much by questions that indeed are legitimate though in the end externally imposed on the texts, but rather will concentrate much more on those themes that are voiced from within the texts themselves. Here as well, one could set one's priorities at various points. I believe, however, that three topics predominate in all of the macroforms of the Hekhalot literature and, therefore, are appropriate as keys to an analysis of its contents: these are the conceptions of God, the angels, and man that the texts provide and the way in which these three "factors" stand in relation to one another.

Every examination of each possible form of Jewish mysticism is confronted with the grandiose synthesis that Gershom Scholem presented in his work. This applies to the Merkavah mysticism of the Hekhalot literature as well. I am concerned primarily with the development of my subject from the sources themselves and do not intend to take as a starting point a discussion with Scholem. Nevertheless, it is suitable to quote Scholem's summarized statements concerning the two central aspects of our subject; namely, the conception of God and man in the Hekhalot literature:

> We are dealing here with a Judaized form of cosmocratorial mysticism.... Not without good reason has Graetz called the religious belief of the Merkabah mystic "Basileomorphism."
>
> This point needs to be stressed, for it makes clear the enormous gulf between the gnosticism of the Hekhaloth and that of the Hellenistic mystics.... In the

Hekhaloth, God is above all King, to be precise, Holy King. This conception reflects a change in the religious consciousness of the Jews—not only the mystics—for which documentary evidence exists in the liturgy of the period. The aspects of God which are really relevant to the religious feeling of the epoch are His majesty and the aura of sublimity and solemnity which surrounds him.

On the other hand, there is a complete absence of any sentiment of divine immanence. . . . The fact is that the true and spontaneous feeling of the Merkabah mystic knows nothing of divine immanence; the infinite gulf between the soul and God the King on His throne is not even bridged at the climax of mystical ecstasy.

Not only is there for the mystic no divine immanence, there is also no love of God. . . . Ecstasy there was, and this fundamental experience must have been a source of religious inspiration, but we find no trace of a mystical union between the soul and God. Throughout there remained an almost exaggerated consciousness of God's *otherness*. . . . The magnificence and majesty of God, on the other hand, this experience of the *Yorede Merkabah* which overwhelms and overshadows all the others, is not only heralded but also described with an abundance of detail and almost to excess. . . . *Majesty, Fear* and *Trembling* are indeed the key-words to this Open Sesame of religion.[29]

---

[29]*Major Trends in Jewish Mysticism,* pp. 54–56.

2

Hekhalot Rabbati

God

God as King upon His Throne

If one reads the macroform known as *Hekhalot Rabbati* in its context, then there can be no doubt as to the sheer overwhelmingly dominant aspect of the conception of God presented in *Hekhalot Rabbati:* God is enthroned as king upon his throne.[1] The location of this throne is according to the classical geography of the Hekhalot literature, which here is more presumed than specified, the "palace"

[1]Mostly on the "throne of glory" of Jeremiah 14:21 and 17:12; less often on the "high and sublime throne" of Isaiah 6:1. The prophetic reports of visions from Isaiah 6 and Ezekiel 1–10 (cf. Ezekiel 1:26; 10:1) are thereby taken up and elaborated on.

(*hekhal*) in the highest, that is, seventh heaven: "Because upon a high and sublime, frightful and terrible throne do you reside, in the chambers of the sublime palace."[2] The throne was created before God created the world (this is good rabbinic theology),[3] it is God's residence in the world:

> Your throne is a hovering throne
> since the hour
> when you fastened the weaver's peg
> and wove the fabric,[4]
> upon which the completion [of the] world
> and its ladder stand,
> many years and generations without end.
> And he still does not let his feet rest upon
> the ground of the *ʿarevot raqiaʿ*,
> but like a hovering bird
> he rises underneath you.[5]

God swears by "the throne of my splendor, in which consists my honor, which I [have] not left since it was created, and [will not leave] in eternity."[6]

The throne, therefore, is the visible sign of divine power, it is often personified and spoken to directly. In a highly poetic passage we read:

---

[2]Section 153; cf. also sections 157 and 322; further sections 206, 245, 298. The terminology is not completely clear. *Hekhalot Rabbati* speaks explicitly only of seven palaces, not of seven *reqiʿim,* i.e. "heavens" (MS New York 8128 even knows of 390, respectively 80 *reqiʿim*). On the other hand, the idea of seven *reqiʿim* is characteristic of 3 Enoch (sections 15, 21, 29, 33, 41, 42) and of *Reʾuyyot Yeḥezqel* (lines 33, 39, 43, 45, 108 of Gruenwald's edition in *Temirin I,* pp. 103–129); concerning the *Reʾuyyot Yeḥezqel,* which will not be considered in this book, cf. *Hekhalot-Studien,* pp. 8ff.

[3]Together with the Torah; cf. BerR 1,4 and parallels. See A. Goldberg, "Schöpfung und Geschichte. Der Midrasch von den Dingen, die vor der Welt erschaffen wurden," *Judaica* 24 (1968): 27–44; P. Schäfer, "Zur Geschichtsauffassung des rabbinischen Judentums," *JSJ* 6 (1975): 167–188 = idem, *Studien zur Geschichte und Theologie des rabbinischen Judentums,* Leiden, 1978 [AGAJU 15], pp. 26ff.

[4]On the notion of the world as fabric in rabbinic literature, cf. y Pes 4,1, fol. 30d.; MHG Gen p. 12 (ed. Margulies). See B. Murmelstein, "Spuren altorientalistischer Einflüsse im rabbinischen Schrifttum. Die Spinnerinnen des Schicksals," *ZAW* 81 (1969): 217ff.; S. Lieberman, *Tosefta ki-fshutah,* vol. 4, New York, 1962, pp. 772f.; Schäfer, *Studien zur Geschichte und Theologie des rabbinischen Judentums,* pp. 17ff.

[5]Section 98, MS Vatican.

[6]Section 119.

Rejoice, rejoice, supernal dwelling!
Shout, shout for joy, precious vessel![7]
Made marvelously and a marvel!
Gladden, gladden the king who sits upon you! . . .
—for your conversation is with the conversation of your king,
and with your creator do you speak . . . [8]

The throne is closer to God than all other beings (also closer than the angels), its distinction over and above all other beings is based on its having, so to speak, direct access to God, that it can speak with God directly:

And three times daily,
the throne of glory prostrates itself before you
and speaks to you:
ZHRRY'L, Lord, God of Israel,
be honored!
Magnificent king,
sit down upon me,
as your burden is dear to me and not heavy . . . [9]

Its hymn is the climax of the heavenly song of praise:

Like the voice of the seas,
like the roaring of the rivers,
like the waves of Tarshish,
which the south wind drives forward,
like the voice of the hymn of the throne of glory,
which calls to mind and extols
the magnificent king
[with] loud voice and extremely great roaring.
Voices rush away from him,
the throne of glory,

---

[7]The biblical phrase ***keli ḥemdah*** (cf. Jeremiah 25:34; Hosea 13:15; Nahum 2:10; 2 Chronicles 32:27) serves in rabbinical literature above all as a term for the Torah (cf. m Av 3,14) and in the Hekhalot literature, it is evidently conciously assigned to the throne of glory. A noteworthy exception is section 173, where God speaks of his ***ḥayyot*** (see below, p. 22) as "precious vessel"; there, however, the connection is unclear.

[8]Sections 94, 154, 634, 687, cf. also section 686.

[9]Section 99.

to help him,
to strengthen him,
when he calls to mind and praises
the mighty of Jacob,
as is written: 'Holy, holy, holy' (Isaiah 6:3).[10]

In view of such and similar texts it is surely not an exaggeration to speak of a distinct theology of the divine throne in *Hekhalot Rabbati*. The importance of the throne obviously was carried so far that it threatened to abolish the distance between God and his throne, so that the danger arose as it were, of substituting, the throne for God himself.[11] Although it is surely to be understood metaphorically when it is stated: "you shall reign eternally, your throne will reign in all generations,"[12] the problems surrounding such a statement were nonetheless well-known. Otherwise one would have not deemed it necessary to state immediately thereafter: "Be exalted over the palace of eminence, be exalted over those splendidly crowned, . . . be more glorious than all creatures, be honored beyond the throne of your glory, be appreciated more than your precious vessel."[13] It is not by chance that it is said of the *yorede merkavah* who step forth in front of the throne of glory in the seventh palace that they "bring forth all kinds of praises and hymns in front of him" (i.e. the throne).[14] The throne, as an object of worship, has become almost independent; and therefore, it must expressly be remarked that God deserves more honor and praise than his throne.

The kingdom of God is the object of numerous hymns in *Hekhalot Rabbati,*[15] which in a litanylike manner praise God as king.[16]

---

[10]Section 162; cf. also section 161.

[11]The throne perhaps became the object of the vision and speculation out of the desire to avoid the danger of a broader visualization of the enthroned divinity; cf. the dictum of R. Aḥa in b Ḥag 13a: "There is a further *raqia*ʿ above the heads of the creatures, as is written: Above the heads of the creatures was something which looked like a *raqia*ʿ, like an awe-inspiring gleam as of crystal (Ezekiel 1:22). Thus far are you allowed to speak; from here and further on you are not allowed to speak, for it is written in the Book of Ben Sira: Do not explore that which is concealed from you; do not expound that which is hidden from you. Think about that which is permitted to you, but do not occupy yourself with mysteries (Sirach 3:22)."

[12]Section 257.

[13]Ibid.

[14]Section 236.

[15]Cf. sections 165, 193ff., 217, 249, 252ff., 276.

[16]On the linguistic form of the hymns in the Hekhalot literature, cf. especially J.

The form of these litanies is for the most part very simple: the constant "king" is provided with various epithets (whereby at most, an alphabetic acrostic is used as a stylistic means). For example: "King of Israel, beloved king, praised king, king of pride [= proud king], eminent king, . . . decorated king, venerable king, pure king, one and only king, great king, consuming king, splendid king, redeeming king, honored king, protective king, valiant king, passionate king."[17] The highest task of all creatures is to recognize and to praise God as king:

> For [it] is the duty of all creatures
> to make you mighty,
> to adorn you,
> to glorify you,
> to praise you,
> to extol you,
> to make you great,
> to sanctify you,
> to elevate you,
> to embellish you,
> to make you exalted,
> to laud you,
> great and holy king,
> ruler over those above and those below,
> over the first and the last,
> who out of fear and trembling
> sanctify you with a threefold sanctification,
> so, as is written:
> Holy, holy, holy [Isaiah 6:3).[18]

The Appearance of God

Now, if one asks concretely about the appearance of God on his throne (how is God as enthroned king described? is he at all more closely described?), the findings are rather meager. As rich as

---

Maier, "Serienbildung und 'numinoser' Eindruckseffekt in den poetischen Stücken der Hekhalot-Literatur," *Semitics* 3 (1973): 36–66.

[17]Section 217, MS New York; cf. also sections 249, 255.

[18]Section 274.

the text is in endless, at times tiresome, epithets in praising God's kingdom, so reserved is it when it comes to describing God more specifically.[19] For the most part, three aspects are dominant and closely connected with one another.

First, God is overwhelmingly beautiful. This is valid for most of the Hekhalot texts and has flowed into the formula derived from Isaiah 33:17, that the Merkavah mystic desires "to behold the king in his beauty" (*lir'ot et ha-melekh be-yofyo*).[20]

Second, God's beauty is concentrated above all on his countenance (*panim*):[21]

Lovely countenance,
adorned countenance,
countenance of beauty,
countenance of flame[s]
is the countenance of the Lord, the God of Israel,
when he sits upon the throne of his glory. . . .
His beauty is more lovely
than the beauty of the *gevurot;*
his embellishment is more exquisite
than the embellishment of the bridegroom and bride[22]
in the house of their wedding.[23]

The beauty of the divine countenance is so overwhelming that it has a destructive effect upon the observer:

He who looks at him
will immediately be torn;

[19]The *Shi'ur Qomah* tradition (cf. below, pp. 60 and 99ff.) plays no role in *Hekhalot Rabbati;* it is only interpolated, very fragmentarily, in section 167.

[20]Cf. sections 198 (here expressly "to behold the king and the throne"); 248, 259 (here as well "the king and his throne"). Isaiah 33:17 relates an event from the time to come which the Hekhalot literature transfers to the present time: the *yored merkavah* experiences God's beauty in the here and now. On the immediate eschatology of *Hekhalot Rabbati* see below, pp. 42f.

[21]With this as well, an important biblical motif has been absorbed; cf. Exodus 33:18ff. (see below, pp. 57ff); Psalms 11:7; Psalms 42:3. Cf. in rabbinic theology the phrase "to receive the countenance of the Shekhinah"; see A. Goldberg, *Untersuchungen über die Vorstellung von der Schekhinah in der frühen rabbinischen Literatur,* Berlin, 1969 [SJ 5], pp. 292ff.

[22]On the metaphor of the bride and bridegroom, cf. also sections 94, 154, 687.

[23]Section 159.

he who views his beauty
will immediately be poured out like a jug.[24]

If one could here assume that this is true of all observers, that God's beauty is in principle "unbearable," the continuation of the text makes it unequivocally clear as to who is unable to bear God's beauty:

Those who serve him today
will no longer serve him tomorrow,
and those who serve him tomorrow
will no longer serve him [today],
for their strength disappears
and their faces become obscure,
their hearts are led astray,
and their eyes become darkened
due to the embellishment
of the radiance of the beauty of their king . . . [25]

Therefore, it is God's direct servants, the angels, who cannot observe his beauty without perishing, as is confirmed by other passages I shall return to later.[26] Based on the formula mentioned earlier that the Merkavah mystic longs for and is called upon "to behold the king in his beauty," this statement doubtlessly acquires a polemical gist. Man, in contrast to the angels, can (and should) observe God's countenance:

A heavenly punishment [shall befall] you,
you who descend to the Merkavah,
if you do not report and say,
what you have heard,
and if you do not testify,
what you have seen upon the countenance:
countenance of majesty and might,
of pride and eminence,
which elevates itself,

---

[24] Ibid. Cf. also the end of section 356 (*Hekhalot Zuṭarti*) and sections 102 (below, p. 19) and 104 (below, p. 26).

[25] Ibid.

[26] Sections 184, 189, below, pp. 47ff.

which raises itself,
which rages [and] shows itself great.
The countenance shows itself mighty and great
three times daily in the heights,
and no man perceives and knows it,
so, as is written:
Holy, holy, holy (Isaiah 6:3).[27]

This text is notable in several respects. It renders the countenance of God the goal of the *yored merkavah* and simultaneously revokes this statement in a paradoxical way by stressing at the conclusion that one (man) cannot "perceive" this countenance. The *yored merkavah,* nonetheless, does see and "perceive" it, for he is called upon to give an account of it. For him, the countenance of God is namely not only of overwhelming beauty, and, therefore, of a destructive nature, but at the same time the center of a divine event that is obviously of great importance for both the Merkavah mystic and the people on earth to whom he is to report. To a certain degree, everything worthy of seeing and knowing, everything God wishes to transmit to the *yored merkavah,* and that he should further pass on to his fellows is concentrated in God's countenance.

What exactly occurs on God's countenance is not related, though the context leaves no doubt that it is concerned with the heavenly liturgy. The terms *majesty, might, pride* and *eminence* in connection with the verb *to rage* always refer to occurrences that take place in front of the throne of glory,[28] and the mention of "three times daily" clearly illustrates a liturgical event. The application of this well-established terminology to God's countenance apparently is to be understood as stating that God is responding, to a certain degree, to the liturgical event taking place in heaven, that the heavenly liturgy is an interaction between God and those who praise him (the heavenly "forces" in their furthest—cosmic—sense), and that the *yored merkavah* "reads" from the countenance of God the effect of this all-embracing praise.

Third, apart from the countenance of God as the center of all occurrences, only one attribute is accentuated that likewise belongs

[27]Section 169.
[28]Cf. sections 200, 216, 227.

to the context of the kingdom; namely, the divine garment (more precisely the "shirtlike robe": *ḥaluq*):[29]

Measure of holiness,
measure of might,
frightful measure,
terrible measure,
measure of trembling,
measure of shaking,
measure of terror,
measure of vibration,
[that emanates] from the garment of ZHRRY'L,[30]
the Lord, the God of Israel,
who comes crowned to the throne of his glory.[31]

This particular royal garment is covered from top to bottom, "from the inside and from the outside,"[32] with the tetragram YHWH. This apparently is the reason why no creature can look at the garment without incurring injury, as is emphasized:

Of no creature are the eyes
able to observe it,
not the eyes [of a human being] of flesh and blood,
and not the eyes of his servants.
But one who does observe,
beholds exactly and sees it,
his eyeballs are seized and contorted,
and his eyeballs flash
and shoot forth torches of fire.

---

[29]On God's garment, which in rabbinic literature is connected to the creation of light, cf. BerR 1,6; 3,4; ShemR 15,22; PRE ch. 3, fol 7bf. (ed. Warsaw 1851–52) and more often; see V. Aptowitzer, "Zur Kosmologie der Agada. Licht als Urstoff," *MGWJ* 72 (1928): 363–370; A. Altmann, "A Note on the Rabbinic Doctrine of Creation," *JJS* 7 (1956): 195–206; P. Schäfer, "Berēšīt bārā' 'Ĕlōhīm. Zur Interpretation von Genesis 1,1 in der rabbinischen Literatur," *JSJ* 2 (1971): 165f.; Scholem, *Jewish Gnosticism*, pp. 58ff.

[30]The name is likely to be derived from *zohar* ("splendor").

[31]Section 102.

[32]Ibid.

And they scorch him
and they burn him. . . . [33]

Because the reference here is explicitly to angels and men, this text rivals the one cited earlier, in which the *yored merkavah* is called upon to report to his fellows what he saw on God's countenance. One is well-advised not to harmonize these two texts too hastily, but rather to view the tension between the "ability to see" (or "wanting to see") God's beauty on his throne and the danger that arises from this seeing as one of the fundamental statements of *Hekhalot Rabbati* and the Hekhalot literature as a whole (at least on the level of the Ashkenazi redaction as represented by the extensive manuscripts).

The conception of God in *Hekhalot Rabbati* is outlined for the most part through the described aspects of God's kingdom. It is true that in a small number of passages, the Shekhinah also is mentioned;[34] however, the meaning of these passages remains fully unexplained and obscure.[35] The only thing that seems certain is that the phrases have little in common with the rabbinical conception of the Shekhinah.[36] In contrast, of greater importance is the name of God that the angels pronounce,[37] and that—together with the names of the angels—above all finds magical use in the adjuration.[38]

---

[33]Ibid.; cf. also section 105.

[34]Sections 154, 156, 185, cf. also the "Ophannim of the Shekhinah" in sections 198 and 247.

[35]Section 154: the angels "excite" the Shekhinah; section 156: they "camp" in the Shekhinah. On the "camp of the Shekhinah" in rabbinic literature, cf. the analysis of the corresponding passages in Goldberg, *Schekhinah,* pp. 103ff. The term denotes the part of the sanctuary (the holy of holies), in which the Shekhinah "resides." The notion that the angels camp "in the Shekhinah," however, is unique. What perhaps is meant is that they dwell with the Shekhinah in the innermost circle of the divine chambers. Section 185 (in *Hekhalot Rabbati* only in MS New York 8128; in MS Oxford 1531 [section 795] the text belongs to *Seder Rabba di-Bereshit*) is the only passage in *Hekhalot Rabbati* in which the Shekhinah possibly denotes God seated on the throne of glory: "because the Merkavah [lies] upon [their; i.e., the *ḥayyot*) backs and the throne of glory is high above their heads and [the] Shekhinah is above them."

[36]Different is section 297, which refers to the dwelling of the Shekhinah in the temple in the traditional rabbinic diction. This section belongs to the *sar ha-torah* passage that begins in section 281; see *Hekhalot-Studien,* pp. 212f.

[37]Sections 165, 166: the name with which heaven and earth were created; sections 168, 306.

[38]See below, p. 53.

The dominant names of God in *Hekhalot Rabbati* are TWTRWSY'Y (in different variations)[39] and ZHRRY'L.[40]

Angels

Hekhalot Rabbati, as opposed to 3 Enoch for example, shows no disposition toward a systematic angelology. Different aspects are incorporated beside one another and at times in contrast to one another; any attempt to harmonize them would have little success.

The Bearers of the Throne

In view of the pronounced theology of the divine throne, it comes as no surprise that a principal task of the angels is the bearing of the throne of glory. They often are addressed as the "bearers" or "servants" of the throne,[41] whereas it is presumed that not all angels are meant, but rather one privileged group:

The proudest of the proud,
those crowned with crowns
and all kings of the heads of the *middot,*
which you created,
[all of them] stand crowded
under the throne of your glory.
They lift it high
with powerful strength and might.[42]

For how heroic are they,
who carry the throne of this mighty king!
They stand burdened
day and night,
in the evening and in the morning and at noon,
worried,
confused,

---

[39]Cf. sections 172, 195, 196, 204, 206, 216, 218, 219, 252, 257, 266, 267, 301. The name is likely to be derived from *tetras,* i.e., four (namely, the four letters of the tetragram); cf. Y. Levy, *'Olamot nifgashim,* Jerusalem, 1960, p. 263.

[40]Cf. sections 96, 99, 102, 110, 111, 119, 120, 121, 195, 231, 251.

[41]Sections 94, 98, 103, 153, 154, 160, 167, 168, 172, 173, 185, 187f., 189.

[42]Sections 98ff.

frightened,
trembling,
shaking,
fearful.[43]

The *ḥayyot ha-qodesh*

God and his servants live in complete harmony with one another: "Happy the king, for these are his servants. Happy the servants, for this is their king."[44] A particularly important role is played by the four holy creatures of Ezekiel 1:5ff (*ḥayyot ha-qodesh,* "holy creatures"), who in the form of a man, an ox, a lion, and an eagle[45] stand directly beneath the throne:

Every day
when the dawn approaches,
[the] adorned king sits
and blesses the *ḥayyot:*
To you, *ḥayyot,* do I speak,
before you, creatures, do I make myself heard,
ḥayyot, ḥayyot,
who carry the throne of my glory,
with all [your] heart and with desirous soul:
Blessed is the hour
[in which] I created you;
exalted is the constellation
under which I formed you. . . . [46]

This text is to be joined by another, which goes even a step further:

Every day
when the Minḥah prayer approaches,
[the] adorned king sits
and praises the *ḥayyot.*
Even before the speech from his mouth is completed,

---

[43]Section 168. In section 160 an attempt to describe the movement of the Merkavah.

[44]Section 160.

[45]Section 273.

[46]Section 173.

the *ḥayyot ha-qodesh* come forth
under the throne of glory,
from their mouths the fullness of rejoicing,
with their wings the fullness of exaltation;
their hands play [instruments]
and their feet dance;
they walk around and surround their king,
one from the right and one from the left,
one from in front and one from behind.
They embrace and kiss him
and reveal their countenance;
they reveal,
but the king of glory covers his countenance.
And the *ʿarevot raqiaʿ* is torn asunder
in front of the embellishment,
the radiance,
the beauty,
the form,
the wish,
the longing,
[and] desire
[for the] brilliance
of the tiara,
in which the view of their countenance [appears] . . . [47]

This text in part is difficult to understand. However, the presumed situation is clear: the concern is the Minḥah prayer of the *ḥayyot* in front of God on his throne, whereby in the text quoted earlier, the morning prayer obviously is being referred to. The *ḥayyot*'s worship thereby takes on thoroughly physical dimensions, which are reminiscent of human courtship. The climax of this courtship is the alternate revealing and covering of the countenance. During the Minḥah prayer the *ḥayyot* reveal their faces while God covers his own, and during the morning prayer God reveals his face while the *ḥayyot* cover their own.[48] In any case, when God covers his face (during the Minḥah prayer), the *ḥayyot* are consumed with "longing" and

[47]Section 189.

[48]Sections 183f. On the reason why God reveals his countenance precisely during the morning prayer and not during the Minḥah prayer, see below, p. 48 and note 163.

"desire," which finds expression (and its fulfillment?) in the threefold "holy" of the *Qedushah*. Even if one does not wish to go as far as D. Halperin, who presumes massive sexual implications here and in similar passages,[49] one must admit that we are dealing with a very intimate scene.[50]

The Heavenly Praise

Although no systematic angelology was developed in *Hekhalot Rabbati,* as mentioned earlier, there can be no doubt that the *ḥayyot* stand at the top of the angelic hierarchy.[51] The most important task of all angels, regardless of the group to which they belong, is reciting the daily praise in front of God. Large sections of *Hekhalot Rabbati* deal with this praise, which always culminates in the *Qedushah*.[52] The heavenly praise is all-embracing and of sheer cosmic dimension:

> Rivers of joy,
> rivers of delight,
> rivers of exaltation,
> rivers of pleasure,
> rivers of love,
> rivers of friendship
> pour out and go forth
> from in front of the throne of glory.
> They rise and flow

[49]"A Sexual Image in Hekhalot Rabbati and its Implications," in J. Dan (ed.), *Proceedings of the First International Conference on the History of Jewish Mysticism: Early Jewish Mysticism,* Jerusalem, 1987 [JSJT 6, 1–2], pp. 117ff.

[50]Cf. also section 276: "king of the kings of kings, . . . before whom the *ḥayyot* set themselves up and stand whispering. They are fire, their fondness is fire, their gait is fire, their speech is fire. . . . They surround you and are yours, they encircle you, near you they are hidden, in your chambers [literally, in your nests] they reflect on mystery and reason, belted with strength, covered with embellishment."

[51]In *Hekhalot Rabbati* the groups of angels known from Ezekiel 1 and 10 dominate; i.e., the Keruvim, the Ophannim, and above all the *ḥayyot*.

[52]Although the trishagion from Isaiah 6:3 must not necessarily be the *Qedushah* in the technical sense. This is true especially of the so-called Qedushah songs (sections 94–106 and 152–169), in which the trishagion is more likely a means of formally structuring the text; cf. the unpublished masters thesis by L. Renner, "Qedusha und Hekhalot: Zum Verhältnis von synagogaler Liturgie und früher jüdischer Mystik," Berlin, 1989, pp. 59ff.

into the paths of the gates of the *ʿarevot raqiaʿ*:
from the sound of the harp playing of his *ḥayyot*,
from the rejoicing sound of the tambourine of his Ophannim
[and] from the sound of the cymbal playing of his Keruvim
there rises a sound
and goes forth with great roaring
in holiness . . . [53]

It is self-evident that the heavenly praise is directed solely toward God, who is described in a beautifully poetic phrase as being "adorned with the embroidery of the song" (*mehuddar be-riqme shir*).[54] For all others who hear it—men as well as angels—it can be destructive. The following text once again (as in the vision of God)[55] points to the paradox that one cannot really see God nor hear the heavenly praise, although the *yored merkavah* does indeed see God and hears the heavenly praise; thus to the inherent ambivalence of "both . . . as well as" in the texts. The "worthy" *yored merkavah* survives the danger stemming from this praise, the "unworthy" adept is annihilated:

The voice of the first one:
One who hears [this] voice,
will immediately go mad
and tumble down.

The voice of the second one:
Everyone who hears it,
immediately goes astray
and does not return.

The voice of the third one:
One who hears [this] voice,
is struck by cramps
and he dies immediately.

The voice of the fourth one:
Everyone who hears it,

---

[53]Section 161.
[54]Section 252.
[55]See above, pp. 15ff.

the skull of his head and his body is immediately split into
pieces,
and most of the tips of his ribs will be torn off.

The voice of the fifth one:
Everyone who hears it,
will be poured out like a jug[56]
and be completely dissolved in blood.

The voice of the sixth one:
Everyone who hears it,
his heart will immediately be struck by pangs,
and his heart will shake his entrails and whirl [them] around,
and his gall will dissolve in his insides
and will be like water . . . [57]

The angels' own praise, however, also can be dangerous to themselves; namely, when it is not recited as is required of them. *Hekhalot Rabbati* here takes up the rabbinical tradition of the *creatio continua* of the angels as a means to the uninterrupted praise[58] and interprets it to show that the angels' recital of the praise must be absolutely harmonious; any departure from the perfect harmony is punished:

Therefore, they set about
and stimulate
and shine
and gather
in fear,
purity and holiness,
and they intone
hymn,

---

[56]Cf. also section 159 (above, pp. 16f).

[57]Section 104.

[58]Cf. BerR 78,1; Yalq *wayyishlaḥ*, section 133, p. 81a bottom (ed. Jerusalem 1966–67); EkhaR 3,8: "They are renewed every morning (Lamentations 3:23). . . . R. Ḥelbo said: Every day, the Holy One, blessed be he, creates a band of new angels who utter a new song before him and then pass away." There follows a discussion about where they go. The answer is in the river of fire (*nehar dinur*), from which they were created. The *Hekhalot Rabbati* text obviously alludes to this in what follows. Cf. also P. Schäfer, *Rivalität zwischen Engeln und Menschen. Untersuchungen zur rabbinischen Engelvorstellung*, Berlin and New York, 1975 [SJ 8], pp. 54f.

praise and song,
eulogy and tribute
with one voice,
with one speech,
with one knowledge,
with one sound.
And not only this,
but there fall thousands and thousands,
myriads and myriads
into the river of fire[59] and are burned,
as there [can] be no earlier or later,
no lower or higher for them,
when they sing hymn and sanctification
before the king of the kings of kings.
Therefore, each one who [joins in] earlier or later
than his companion will be burned.[60]

The sole exemption from this hazardous destiny are the *ḥayyot ha-qodesh* as bearers of the divine throne. They are so perfect that all of their movements and hymns always are performed in faultless harmony:

But from the[61] *ḥayyot ha-qodesh*
none joins in too early or too late,
for the dimension of their stature is the same,
their thickness is the same,
their wings are the same,
their size is the same,
the crown of their heads is the same,[62]
their radiance is the same
and their beauty is the same.
They are aligned in fours like one,
towards the feet of the throne,
opposite one another:
One *galgal* opposite the other,

---

[59]According to the manuscripts New York 8128 and Munich 22.

[60]Sections 185f.; cf. also sections 306, 334 and section 58 (3 Enoch), below, pp. 131f.

[61]According to most manuscripts.

[62]According to MSS New York and Munich 22.

one Ophan opposite the other,
one *ḥayyah* opposite the other,
one Keruv opposite the other Keruv,
one Seraph opposite the other,
one wing opposite the other,
one harmony opposite the other harmony.
And they open their mouth
in a great hymn,
with fright,
with trembling and shuddering,
with fear and terror,
in purity and holiness
and with the soft murmuring sound,
as is written:
after the earthquake[63] [came the] soft murmuring sound
[1 Kings 19:12].[64]

Individual Angels

Apart from the general names of the various groups of angels (servants, Ophannim, Keruvim, Seraphim, *galgalim, ḥayyot,* etc.), a number of particular angels are given special prominence, as individuals, so to speak. Although it is not possible to place them in a hierarchical relation to one another, there is no doubt that we are dealing with especially prominent angels.

The Angel of the Countenance. In two passages, an "angel of the countenance" (*malʾakh ha-panim*) is mentioned. The term is biblical [65] and to be differentiated from the more frequently mentioned "Prince of the Countenance" (*sar ha-panim*).[66] The function of the angel of the countenance is not wholly clear. We learn only that he is present when God descends from the *raqiaʿ* over the heads of the *ḥayyot;* therefore, apparently from the eighth heaven to the seventh

---

[63]MT: "fire."

[64]Section 187. The text belongs to a unit of traditions that alone in MS New York 8128 is integrated in *Hekhalot Rabbati;* in MSS Oxford 1531 and Munich 22 it belongs to *Seder Rabba di-Bereshit.* Obviously here the emphasis lies much more strongly on the angelic liturgy, and the redactor of MS New York incorporated this unit into the reports of ascension.

[65]Isaiah 63:9 (*malʾakh panaw*).

[66]Cf. below, p. 36.

heaven[67] where his throne stands.[68] It is concretely stated of him that he prepares the throne for God ("when the angel of the countenance enters, to order beautifully the throne of his glory and to prepare the seat for the noble of Jacob")[69] and, strangely enough, that he "binds" crowns and sets them on the heads of the angels that stand around the throne and prostrates himself in front of them. He, therefore, appears to be something like the supreme master of ceremonies, who prepares everything for the descent of God to his throne.

Meṭaṭron. Meṭaṭron,[70] known from the majority of the Hekhalot texts and rabbinic writings[71] as the heavenly angelic prince par excellence (cf. 3 Enoch in particular), plays only a subordinate role in *Hekhalot Rabbati.* He functions, together with other angels, as Yishmaᶜel's angel of revelation and Israel's intercessor.[72] In addition,

---

[67]Cf. Ezekiel 1:22f.; and Gruenwald, *Apocalyptic and Merkavah Mysticism,* pp. 153f.

[68]Section 100.

[69]Section 170. It is surely no coincidence that in the previous paragraph (169) God's countenance is described.

[70]Numerous speculations have been made concerning the meaning of the name Meṭaṭron; cf. above all H. Odeberg, *3 Enoch or the Hebrew Book of Enoch,* Cambridge, 1928 (reprint New York, 1973), pp. 125ff.; Scholem, *Major Trends in Jewish Mysticism,* pp. 69–70; P. S. Alexander, "The Historical Setting of the Hebrew Book of Enoch," *JJS* 28 (1977): 162; S. Lieberman, "Metatron, the Meaning of His Name and His Functions" (Appendix), in Gruenwald, *Apocalyptic and Merkavah Mysticism,* pp. 235ff. Most probable is the etymology of Lieberman: Meṭaṭron = Greek *metatronos* = *metathronos* = *synthronos;* i.e., the small "minor god," whose throne is beside that of the great "main God." The spelling *Miṭaṭron,* especially in the early manuscripts, does not contradict this derivation (so Alexander, ibid.), because the rendering of the *Shewa* with *Yod* is quite normal.

[71]Cf. b San 38b; b Ḥag 15a; b AZ 3b; Targum Ps-Jon Genesis 5:24; 34:6. *Metatron* also is mentioned repeatedly in the Babylonian magic bowls; cf. C. H. Gordon, "Two Magic Bowls in Teheran," *Orientalia* 20 (1951): 307, l.5; idem., "Aramaic Magical Bowls in the Istanbul and Baghdad Museums," *Archiv Orientální* 6 (1934): 328, D/11; idem., "Aramaic and Mandaic Magical Bowls," *Archiv Orientální* 9 (1937): 94, L/12–13; W. S. McCullough, *Jewish and Mandean Incantation Texts in the Royal Ontario Museum,* Toronto, 1967, D/5–6; J. A. Montgomery, *Aramaic Incantation Texts from Nippur,* Philadelphia, 1913, No. 25/4; C. D. Isbell, *Corpus of Aramaic Incantation Bowls,* Missoula, Mont., 1975, Texts 34, 49, 56, and 57; M. J. Geller, "Two Incantation Bowls Inscribed in Syriac and Aramaic," *BSOAS* 39 (1976): 422–427, Aramaic Bowl B/10.

[72]See below, p. 36 (angels of revelation) and pp. 33ff. (intercessors).

the traditions of his special names[73] and his elevation[74] are incorporated in *Hekhalot Rabbati,* and one can assume that they are not necessarily "original" here.[75] In one passage alone, which speaks of the *ʾeved* ("servant"),[76] Meṭaṭron seems to be integrated in the style and diction of *Hekhalot Rabbati;* however, the connection is difficult to understand. The context is apparently that the "servant," that is, Meṭaṭron (?), shrinks from the service in the immediate vicinity of God.

ʿAnafiʾel. In contrast, the angel ʿAnafiʾel appears to be characteristic especially of *Hekhalot Rabbati* (though he is also mentioned in other texts). His name is uttered three times daily in front of the throne of glory; namely, "because the signet ring of heaven and earth is placed in his hand."[77] Other texts state that God prepared or sealed heaven and earth with the signet ring of his hand.[78] If ʿAnafiʾel is the "keeper" of the divine ring of the seal, so to speak, then for *Hekhalot Rabbati* he must belong to the most prominent angels, if not being the most prominent himself. This fits in with the statement made of him that "all [angels] in the heights" prostrate themselves in front of him; "there is nothing in the heights like this," not even the angels who stand in front of the throne of glory; and that God has expressly granted them permission to do so.[79] ʿAnafiʾel functions simultaneously as the guard at the entrance to the seventh palace and possesses the authority to open and close the doors to the seventh palace (in which stands the throne of glory). His unusual

---

73. Sections 277ff.; 310.

74. Sections 148f. = 316f., 295.

75. The conclusion of section 276, and section 277 probably belongs to the unit of traditions that combines *Alpha Beta de-Rabbi ʿAqiva* and *Meṭaṭron* traditions; cf. *Hekhalot-Studien,* pp. 227ff. The sections 278–280 are marked as "supplement" in MS Budapest 238 and apparently constitute the transition to the *sar ha-torah* passage that begins with section 281. Section 310 belongs to a separate macroform, which begins with section 307 (in numerous manuscripts the macroform *Hekhalot Rabbati* ends with section 306) and that has the title "Chapter of R. Neḥunyah b. Haqanah." The sections 148f. = 316f. are part of a textual unit that is transmitted only in the manuscripts New York 8128 and Vatican 228 and that is thematically (praise of repentence) completely unique. Section 295 also is part of a passage, marked "supplement," transmitted only in MS Budapest 238.

76. Section 96.

77. Section 241.

78. Cf. sections 320, 389, 396, 833, 840.

79. Section 242.

name ʿAnafiʾel (from *ʿanaf,* "branch") appears to have seemed strange to the transmitters or redactors of the texts and is explained as follows:

> Why is his name ʿAnafiʾel?
> Because of the branch of his crown of crowns,
> which is laid round his head,
> which conceals and covers all the chambers of the palace of the *ʿarevot raqiaʿ*
> like the maker of creation.[80]
>
> What [is special about] the maker of creation?
> [As] the scripture teaches in reference to him:
> His majesty covers the skies [Habakkuk 3:3],
> so does this also apply for the prince ʿAnafiʾel, the servant,
> who is named after the name of his master.[81]

ʿAnafiʾel, therefore, is almost equal to God, and the terminology used here ("servant," "named after the name of his master," i.e., that his name is almost identical to that of God) allows one to assume that qualities have been ascribed to him that otherwise belong only to Meṭaṭron.[82] Whether ʿAnafiʾel should be identified here with Meṭaṭron, and whether this reflects a secondary stage of the tradition, cannot be further pursued in this connection.[83]

---

[80] God.

[81] Section 244; cf. also section 26 (3 Enoch).

[82] Cf. above all 3 Enoch; below, pp. 132ff.

[83] Cf. J. Dan, " ʿAnafiʾel, Meṭaṭron we-yoṣer bereshit," *Tarbiz* 52 1982–83): 447–457. Based on an analysis of the ʿAnafiʾel and Meṭaṭron passages in *Hekhalot Rabbati* and 3 Enoch, Dan reaches the conclusion that behind ʿAnafiʾel is concealed the remains of a figure who is understood to have been a "partner" of God at the time of creation (cf. the term *maker of creation* [*yoṣer bereshit*] in the above quoted text) and who was integrated into the Hekhalot literature, the authors or redactors not having been fully aware of the implications. The figure of Meṭaṭron was also originally conceived in this respect, however, the authors of 3 Enoch, realizing this danger, connected Metatron with the man Enoch, thus domesticating him, so to speak. In the clearly perceivable subordination of Meṭaṭron in relation to ʿAnafiʾel, the original conception of both figures can be detected; namely, their participation in creation. This reconstruction is tempting, however, it does not explain, among other things, how and why both figures came to be connected with one another in the Hekhalot literature. Dan believes that the authors or redactors of the Hekhalot literature then always brought ʿAnafiʾel into play when they needed a figure superior to Meṭaṭron. This means, however, they would have exorcized the devil with Beelzebub, for the

Dumi'el. The angel Dumi'el is also characteristic of *Hekhalot Rabbati,* who like ʿAnafi'el is named after the name of God:

> [The] Lord, the God of Israel,
> named me Dumi'el after his name.
> As I[84] see [and] keep silent
> so [also] Dumi'el.
> His authority is the right doorjamb,[85]
> and he is pushed aside by Qaṣpi'el, the prince.
> He,[86] however, [feels] neither hostility nor hate against him,[87]
> neither jealousy nor rivalry.
> On the contrary: This one to my honor and that one to my honor.[88]

Dumi'el stands together with Qaṣpi'el as gatekeeper at the entrance to the sixth palace. His companion is envious of him—obviously because he is compared directly with God—and pushes him aside from the privileged position at the right side of the entrance;[89] Dumi'el, however, remains silent and thereby is precisely similar to God. Unfortunately, this point is not further explicated; nevertheless, the tradition of the silent (and tolerative = suffering?) God is remarkable enough.[90] In any case, in what follows, Dumi'el kindly

---

"demiurgic qualities" of ʿAnafi'el are nevertheless greater and more evident than those of Meṭaṭron. With ʿAnafi'el, they would have reinstated to a certain extent the proto-Meṭaṭron whose potency they had so successfully deprived through the connection with Enoch.

[84]God: the subject of this text fluctuates between God and Dumi'el.

[85]At the entrance to the sixth palace.

[86]Dumi'el.

[87]Qaṣpi'el. Dumi'el and Qaṣpi'el are fine examples for the way in which the names of the angels can conform to their function or behavior: Dumi'el is derived from DWM/DMM = "to keep silent," Qaṣpi'el from QṢP = "to be angry with."

[88]Section 230.

[89]See in detail my edition of the new *Hekhalot Rabbati* fragment, in *Hekhalot-Studien*, pp. 96ff.

[90]Cf. in rabbinic literature the tradition that God created man against the opposition of the angels and thereby consciously accepted the sins of men (BerR 8,4ff. and parallels; on this Schäfer, *Rivalität,* pp. 90ff.), which is connected in some texts (b San 38b and parallels; on this Schäfer, *Rivalität,* pp. 95ff.) with Isaiah 46:4 ("I was the Maker, and I will be the Bearer; and I will carry and rescue [you]") and which was also adopted by 3 Enoch (section 6). In rabbinic literature, God's silence is the expression of sorrow over the destruction of the temple; cf. PesK 15,3, pp. 250f. (ed. Mandelbaum) = EkhaZ 1,18 (the biblical connecting link is Lamentations

receives the worthy *yored merkavah* and tests him to see if he possesses enough knowledge of the Torah[91] to be allowed to enter the seventh palace.

The Gatekeepers. A special group of angels are the aforementioned gatekeepers at the entrances to the seven palaces. Their enumeration and the careful transmission of their names take up a large portion of *Hekhalot Rabbati.*[92] The seals composed of different names of God and of the "Prince of the Countenance" must be shown to them[93] and their leaders, who stand respectively to the left and right of the threshold, accompany the worthy adepts who have the "correct" seals to the next higher palace. *Hekhalot Rabbati* places great importance on stressing the danger for the *yored merkavah* that emanates from these guardian angels. As is to be expected, this danger is intensified artistically in the description of the seventh palace.[94] As real as this threat is surely meant to be, with its graphic depictions and painstaking details,[95] it would be premature to take it too literally.[96]

Intercessors of Israel. The angels in *Hekhalot Rabbati* are not only God's princely household, and not only there to serve and praise God, but also stand in relation to man. As we have seen, already the task of the gatekeepers at the entrances to the seven palaces is an

---

3:28); b AZ 3b (Isaiah 42:14); PesR 28, fol. 134b (ed. Friedmann); EkhaZ 2,18 (see P. Kuhn, *Gottes Trauer und Klage in der rabbinischen Überlieferung,* Leiden, 1978 [AGAJU 13], pp. 170, 181ff., 215f., 240f., 411f., 477).

[91] See below, pp. 37ff.

[92] Sections 207ff., 241ff.

[93] Sections 219ff.

[94] Sections 213–215: "At the entrance to the seventh palace stand and rage all heros, lordly, powerful and hard, frightening and terrible, who are higher than mountains and more polished than hills. Their bows are strung before the countenance, the swords lie sharpened in their hands. Bolts of lightening shoot forth from their eyeballs, canals of fire from their noses and torches of coal from their mouths. They are adorned [with] helmets and coats of mail, lances and spears hang on their arms. . . . And a cloud is there over their heads, which drips blood over their heads and [the heads] of their horses. This is the sign and measurement of the guardians at the entrance to the seventh palace."

[95] Cf. J. Maier, "Das Gefährdungsmotiv bei der Himmelsreise in der jüdischen Apokalyptik and 'Gnosis'," *Kairos* 1 (1963): 18–40; Schäfer, *Hekhalot-Studien,* pp. 250ff.

[96] See below, p. 39.

ambivalent one: on the one hand, they protect the divine sphere from those who are unauthorized and who attempt to penetrate it; on the other hand, they provide help and support to those who are worthy of seeing God in his beauty. Other texts, however, see the angels functioning exclusively as intercessors of Israel, a well-known motif from early Jewish and rabbinic literature,[97] but rather surprising in the Hekhalot literature:

Those [who] destroy the decree,
who undo [the] oath,
who take away [the] anger,
who assuage [the] jealousy,
who call [the] love to mind,
the love of Abraham, our father,
before their king.

When they see him,
how he is angered with his sons,
what do they [then] do?

They smash their crowns
and loosen their hips
and strike their heads
and fall upon their faces
and speak:
loosen, loosen, maker of creation,
excuse, excuse, noble of Jacob,
pardon, pardon, Israel's holy one,
for you are a powerful one of the kings . . .
Why [do] you [feel] hostility against the seed of Abraham?
Why [do] you [feel] jealousy against the seed of Isaac?
Why [do] you [feel] rivalry against the seed of Jacob?
For a possession of heaven and earth
have you named them.[98]

This emphatic intercession on behalf of Israel (to what it refers remains open, although it is certain that not "only" is the *yored*

[97] Cf. Schäfer, *Rivalität*, pp. 28ff., 62ff.
[98] Sections 190ff.; cf. also section 158.

merkavah meant, but in principle, the relationship between Israel and God) is followed immediately by the divine approbation:

> Then rays[99] go forth
> from underneath the throne of his glory,
> families and families,
> and they blow [the ram's horn]
> and shout and bless:
> Blessed are you,
> who intercede for my sons.
> Be praised,
> [you] who distinguish the fathers.
> And the whole host of the heights
> give them honor and greatness.[100]

Unfortunately, we are not told here which angels actually are being addressed as intercessors of Israel. From the redactional context (the "courtship" of the *ḥayyot* during the Minḥah prayer precedes) perhaps it is not a misleading assumption that we even may be dealing with the *ḥayyot*. This, however, then would be a remarkable gist of the redactor, for it is precisely the *ḥayyot,* as we shall see, who stand in a competitive relationship to Israel for God's love.

Within the apocalyptic passages incorporated into *Hekhalot Rabbati,* we find a strange adaptation of the tradition of the ascent of Enoch = Meṭaṭron.[101] The presumed situation is the banishment of Israel (the actual biblical exile), and Meṭaṭron (who is already located in heaven; Enoch is not mentioned) confers with Mikha'el and Gavri'el as to what should be done and who will dare to ascend to the highest heaven and cry in front of God and plead that he show mercy to Israel. Meṭaṭron's ascent, which the angels attempt in vain to obstruct and which is described in a manner most similar to Enoch's ascent in 3 Enoch,[102] convinces God to show mercy and save Israel despite its sins. It is obvious that we are dealing here with

---

[99]Perhaps the "horns" that are blown are also alluded to; the Hebrew expression *qeren* is very ambivalent (cf. Exodus 34:29 and Daniel 8:6.20). B Hag 13a expressly mentions the "horns" of the *ḥayyot* as well.

[100]Section 192.

[101]Sections 147ff., 315ff.

[102]Section 9.

a later adaptation of the Enoch-Meṭaṭron myth, which in its style and content is fundamentally different from the previously discussed traditions of *Hekhalot Rabbati*.

The Prince of the Torah. Finally, mention also must be made in this connection to the "Prince of the Torah" (*sar ha-torah*), who plays a central role in the section in *Hekhalot Rabbati* named after him, the *sar ha-torah* passage.[103] He is the angelic prince who guards against forgetting the Torah: his "Midrash" can be "learned" and "recited," one adjures him with his names[104] and thereby attains the complete and everlasting knowledge of the Torah.[105]

Angels of Revelation. To a particular literary layer in *Hekhalot Rabbati* belong the angels who function as angels of revelation (in most cases those of R. Yishmaʿel). They are to be found exclusively in the apocalyptic texts incorporated in *Hekhalot Rabbati* that might best be compared to 3 Enoch. These are Suriya;[106] Sasangiʾel;[107] Hadariʾel;[108] Aktariʾel;[109] Meṭaṭron;[110] the voice of Heaven (Bat Qol), which is likewise identical with God and functions here as an angel of revelation;[111] ʾWZHYH;[112] ZGNGʾL.[113] The title that accompanies these angels—with the exception of Aktariʾel, who is named "Lord, God of the host,"[114] and Hadariʾel, who is merely called "prince"[115]—as a rule, is "Prince of the Countenance" (*sar ha-panim*) and thereby places them among the highest classes of angels.

---

[103]Sections 278ff.; section 298: "order of the Prince of the Torah"; section 300: "Midrash of the Prince of the Torah."

[104]The preferred name is apparently Yofiʾel; cf. section 313.

[105]See below, pp. 49ff.

[106]In the story of the ten martyrs: sections 117ff.; Qedushah songs: in section 152 the introductory formula likely is added secondarily, as we are dealing with the seam between the apocalyptic passages and the recommencement of the Qedushah songs.

[107]Apocalypse of David: sections 122ff.

[108]Ibid.: section 124.

[109]*Aggadat R. Yishma*ʿel: section 130. This passage is especially noteworthy, because Aktariʾel here clearly is God himself, who, however, functions as an angel of revelation.

[110]Ibid.: section 131; Messiah Aggadah: section 140; a cosmological passage: section 146.

[111]*Aggadat R. Yishma*ʿel: section 132.

[112]A separate transmitted passage of the story of the ten martyrs: section 139.

[113]Messiah Aggadah: section 145.

[114]Cf. also sections 138, 151, 309, 310.

[115]Hadariʾel otherwise never receives the title *sar ha-panim*.

Man

The *yored merkavah*

In *Hekhalot Rabbati,* man appears above all as the *yored merkavah,* thus as that (exceptional and privileged) person who descends to the Merkavah, the divine chariot. It is no coincidence that the macroform *Hekhalot Rabbati* begins, in all manuscripts and without an introduction, with the following question. "R. Yishmael said: What are the hymns recited by him who wishes to behold the vision of the Merkavah, to descend in peace and to ascend in peace?"[116] Man is primarily the subject of the heavenly journey—though not exclusively, as we shall see. He undertakes the hazardous ascent through the seven *hekhalot,* passing the guardian angels, who, as we have seen, either threaten him or, if he proves himself worthy, help him:

> If he is worthy to descend to the Merkavah—
> If they [the angels] say to him:
> Enter!
> [but] he does not enter [immediately],
> and they once again say to him:
> Enter!
> and he [then] immediately enters,
> [then] they praise him and say:
> Surely this one is [one] of the *yorede merkavah.*
>
> If he however, is not worthy to descend to the Merkavah,
> [and] if they say to him:
> Enter![117]
> and he [then immediately] enters,
> [then] they immediately throw pieces of iron at him.[118]

---

[116] Section 18; on the terminology see above, p. 2, n. 4.

[117] According to the manuscripts Budapest 238 and Leiden 4730; the manuscripts New York 8128, Oxford 1531, Munich 40, Munich 22, Dropsie 436 and Vatican 228 read "do not enter!" and thus strengthen the absurdity of the "test," for the *yored merkavah* enters the *hekhal* despite the angel's warning. In the parallel passage, section 407, all manuscripts read "Enter!"

[118] Section 258.

This test, which obviously is meant to show that the adept is allowed to enter the (sixth)[119] *hekhal* on the second summons only, appears relatively harmless in comparison to another, in which the gatekeepers give the impression that they hurl "thousands upon thousands of waves of water" at the unsuspecting *yored merkavah*. In reality, however, not a single drop of water is there, but only the radiance of the marble stones with which the *hekhal* is furnished.[120] The unworthy adept exposes himself by shouting frightfully: "What is the nature of this water?"[121] whereupon he is immediately punished by having "thousands upon thousands of pieces of iron" thrown at him, and this time for real and not just in his imagination.[122]

---

[119]That the sixth *hekhal* must be meant here follows from the continuation in section 259; cf. also below, p. 65 and n. 55.

[120]Section 259. Cf. the parallels in *Hekhalot Zuṭarti,* sections 345, 407–410.

[121]Ibid.

[122]On the water test, cf. above all Scholem, *Major Trends in Jewish Mysticism,* p. 53 and n. 48; idem, *Jewish Gnosticism,* pp. 14ff.; E. E. Urbach, "Ha-masorot ʿal torat ha-sod bi-tequfat ha-tannaʾim," in *Studies in Mysticism and Religion Presented to G. Scholem,* Jerusalem, 1967, pp. 15f.; A. Goldberg, "Der verkannte Gott. Prüfung und Scheitern der Adepten in der Merkavamystik," *ZRGG* 26 (1974): 17–29; Gruenwald, *Apocalyptic and Merkavah Mysticism,* pp. 87f.; Halperin, *The Merkabah in Rabbinic Literature,* pp. 87f.; Schäfer, *Hekhalot-Studien,* pp. 244ff. A satisfactory explanation of the puzzling waves of water, falsly interpreted by the unworthy *yored merkavah,* has not yet been provided. Whereas Scholem wants rather incidentally to see in the water an illusion to an original ecstatic experience, Goldberg analyzed the texts in more detail and believes that the concern is with the perception of the correct image of God: the unworthy *yored merkavah* "was not worthy to see God, not because he was mistaken, but because he, like those who kissed the calf, had always misperceived God, because he had undertaken the ascent with an already false image of God" ("Der verkannte Gott," p. 29). The false image of God thus is the image of God as the golden calf (to which the texts also refer; cf. sections 259; 408). The correct image of God is that which Moses and the elders saw on Sinai. It appears to me that this explanation is problematic in its assumption; namely, that in the Hekhalot literature the main concern is the "perception of an image": "to see the king in his beauty, to perceive his appearance, that is the goal of this searching and knowledge" (ibid.). As we shall see, it is precisely not so much the image and the appearance that are central in the Hekhalot literature. Recently, Halperin once again considered the texts (*The Faces of the Chariot,* pp. 199ff.). According to him the "water" symbolizes the powers of chaos that God has subdued. Those who associate the divine marble stones with water denounce God, for they insinuate that the powers of chaos remain effective because they have not been finally conquered by God. This ingenious explanation, which has been arrived at through a breathtaking mixture of the most varied sources, deserves a more thorough discussion. Cf. now also R. Reichmann, "Die 'Wasser-Episode' in der Hekhalot-Literatur," *FJB* 17 (1989): 67–100.

As dangerous as the angels appear to the adept who ascends to the divine throne, in reality their power is very limited. Characteristic of this is the much-discussed episode of the gatekeepers who strangely enough annihilate the worthy adepts and allow the unworthy ones to pass unhindered; although they are punished and consumed by fire because of this, their successors behave in exactly the same way.[123] This text almost reads like a parody of the threat that stems from the gatekeepers, and there is some reason to believe that its gist is meant to illustrate exactly this; namely, that the gatekeepers, who are so dangerous and so frightful to look at, in reality are insignificant and that the evaluation of who is deemed worthy or unworthy is not at all dependent on their decision. The decision as to who is worthy to ascend to the Merkavah is obviously made—at least according to a clearly defined redactional layer of *Hekhalot Rabbati*[124]—not at all in heaven but rather already on earth. An essential sign of the worthy *yored merkavah* is his knowledge of the Torah; that is, the question of whether he has proven himself in the explanation and practical application of the Torah, the complete written and oral Torah. He alone is allowed to ascend to the Merkavah "who has read the Torah, prophets and writings, Mishnayot, Midrash, Halakhot and Haggadot and learns the interpretation of the Halakhot, prohibition and permission, who abides by every prohibition that is written in the Torah and observes all the warnings of the laws, statutes and instructions which were said to Moses at Sinai."[125] The Torah knowledge of the worthy *yored merkavah* is written down by the scribal angel Gavri'el and is pinned, as it were, as an entrance ticket to the mast of the wagon with which he enters the seventh *hekhal*.

Therefore, a surprisingly traditional element plays an important role in the heavenly journey of the Merkavah mystic. Nevertheless, it must be stressed that this is only one side of the coin. Simultaneously (and redactionally difficult to separate), the traditional layer is interspersed with elements filled with magic and theurgy (I would even say that these are quantitatively, for certain, and in

---

[123]Sections 224ff. Cf. *Hekhalot-Studien*, pp. 256f., and above all M. Schlüter, "Die Erzählung von der Rückholung des R. Neḥunya ben Haqana aus der *Merkava*-Schau in ihrem redaktionellen Rahmen," *FJB* 10 (1987): 65–109.

[124]The so-called *ḥavurah* report, which begins in section 198.

[125]Section 234.

all probability also qualitatively dominant).[126] The *yored merkavah* not only must show the gatekeepers the correct seals to pass by unhindered, but in the end his entrance ticket, the knowledge of the Torah,[127] also is not enough to enable him to enter the seventh *hekhal*. In any case, the redactor felt it necessary to add at this point: "*Nonetheless,* he must show them (= the gatekeepers of the seventh *hekhal*) the great seal and the frightful crown,"[128] thus magical tools that help him to finally step over the threshold. The reports of the ascent in *Hekhalot Rabbati* thus are mixed with traditional and magical-theurgic elements, which can hardly be separated from one another without running the risk of misinterpreting the text.

The limited power of the angels in connection with the ascent of the *yored merkavah* corresponds to God's appraisal of this ascent. God finds pleasure, as is expressly stated, in those who ascend to the Merkavah; he sits and awaits "each and every one from Israel":

> When does he descend
> in wonderful pride
> and strange power,
> in the pride of elevation
> and [in the] power of sublimity,
> which are excited before the throne of glory
> three times daily in the heights,
> since the world was created
> and till now to praise.[129]

In another passage it is said that ṬWṬRWSY'Y, the Lord, the God of Israel, "longs for and keeps watch, just as he keeps watch for the redemption and for the time of salvation that has been preserved for Israel since the destruction of the second, last temple":

> When will he descend,
> who descends to the Merkavah?

[126] More detailed examinations of the redaction of *Hekhalot Rabbati* perhaps may provide more exact information on the relation between traditional and magical-theurgic elements. It is possible that a composition, originally imbued more strongly by magic, underwent an "orthodox" redaction.

[127] Although the Torah as an entrance ticket also, so to speak, is magically instrumentalized, for it is pinned to the mast of the wagon as an apotropaic tool.

[128] Section 236.

[129] Section 216.

When will he see the pride of the heights?
When will he hear the ultimate salvation?
When will he see,
[what] no eye has [ever] seen?
When will he [again] ascend
and proclaim [this] to the seed of Abraham,
his beloved?[130]

The *yored merkavah* thereby is the favored one, not to say Israel's chosen who undertakes the privilege of the heavenly journey and whose ascent to the throne of glory is passionately awaited by God. A clearly defined literary unit,[131] which is not without reason placed at the beginning of the macroform *Hekhalot Rabbati,* praises the superior greatness of the Merkavah mystic:

The greatest thing of all[132] is the fact
that he sees and recognizes all the deeds of men,
even [those] that they do in the chambers of chambers,
whether they are good or corrupt deeds.

If a man steals,
he knows [it] and recognizes him;
If one commits adultery,
he knows [it] and recognizes him;
If [one] has murdered,
he knows [it] and recognizes him;
If one is suspected of having sexual intercourse with a menstruous woman,
he knows [it] and recognizes him;
If one spreads evil rumors,
he knows [it] and recognizes him. . . . [133]

The greatest thing of all is the fact
that all creatures will be before him
like silver before the silversmith,

---

[130]Section 218.

[131]The so-called *gedullah* passages, sections 81–93. See G. A. Wewers, "Die Überlegenheit des Mystikers. Zur Aussage der Gedulla-Hymnen in Hekhalot-Rabbati 1,2–2,3," *JSJ* 17 (1986): 3–22.

[132]Of the *yored merkavah*.

[133]Section 83.

who perceives
which silver has been refined,
which silver is impure,
and which silver is pure.
He even sees into the families,
how many bastards there are in the family,
how many sons sired during menstruation,
how many with crushed testicles,
how many with mutilated penis,
how many slaves
and how many sons from uncircumcised [fathers].[134]

The Merkavah mystic knows all the deeds of man, the good as well as the bad. In particular, he knows exactly about the purity of the families, he separates, like the silversmith, the pure from the impure, the qualified from the unqualified. The supposition arises that here the "messenger of the Lord" in Malachi 3:1ff. is being alluded to, who prepares the "day of the Lord":

> But who can endure the day of his coming, and who can hold out when he appears? For he is like a smelter's fire and fuller's lye. He shall sit like a smelter and purger of silver, and he shall purify the descendants of Levi and refine them like gold and silver. . . . I will step forward to contend against you, and I will act as a relentless accuser against those who have no fear of me: Who practice sorcery,[135] who commit adultery, who swear falsely, who cheat laborers of their hire, and who subvert [the cause of] the widow, orphan, and stranger, said the Lord of Hosts.[136]

The similarity with regard to the structure as well as the contents of these Malachi verses with the quoted *gedullah* passages from *Hekhalot Rabbati* is unmistakable. If one considers further the accomplished identification of the "messenger of the Lord" with the prophet Elijah as the precursor of the Messiah in Malachi 3:23,

---

[134]Section 86.

[135]At the end of section 83 one of the qualities of the *yored merkavah* emphasized is "that he recognizes all those acquainted with sorcery."

[136]Malachi 3:2–5.

which became part and parcel of rabbinic theology,[137] then the conclusion is not exaggerated that the *yored merkavah* (at least in the so-called *gedullah* passages) is attributed quasi-messianic qualities. The Merkavah mystic takes the place of the Messiah, so to speak, he decides between good and evil, pure and impure. Therefore, it is not surprising that the Messiah and the messianic time and redemption play no major role in *Hekhalot Rabbati* (and, with the exception of 3 Enoch, in the Hekhalot literature as a whole):[138] the *yored merkavah,* in his fullest development in the *gedullah* passages of *Hekhalot Rabbati,* has rendered the Messiah superfluous. The Messiah indeed is mentioned occasionally in *Hekhalot Rabbati;* however, these are always passages that formally are clearly separate from the other texts and that distinctly follow the example of classical apocalyptic traditions.[139]

It is self-evident that this special status of the *yored merkavah* cannot have remained unchallenged. We know next to nothing about the time, location, and social environment of the circles expressing themselves here; nonetheless, the opposition can be read from the *gedullah* passages themselves:

> The greatest thing of all is the fact:
> Who raises a hand against him and strikes him,
> they[140] dress him with plagues,
> they cover him with leprosy,
> they adorn him with a rash.
>
> The greatest thing of all is that fact:
> Who slanders him,
> on him do they throw and cast

[137] Cf. e.g. PesR 35, fol. 161a (ed. Friedmann); PesK 5, pp. 96f. (ed. Mandelbaum); see A. Goldberg, *Ich komme und wohne in deiner Mitte. Eine rabbinische Homilie zu Sacharja 2,14 (PesR 35)*, Frankfurt am Main, 1977 [FJS 3], pp. 60ff.; ShirZ 5,2; WaR 34,8; RuthR 5,6; m Soṭ 9,15; MidrTeh 43,1; Targum Ekha 4,22 (see E. Levine, *The Aramaic Version of Lamentations,* New York, 1976, p. 176); Targum Ps-Jon and Targum Frgm Numbers 25:12; b San 97b–98a.

[138] Therein lies a decisive difference to the classical apocalypses of early Judaism.

[139] Sections 122ff.: Apocalypse of David, *Aggadat R. Yishmaʿel,* Messiah Aggada; see below, p. 44 and n. 145. The redactor who incorporated the apocalyptic material into *Hekhalot Rabbati* perhaps wished to directly create a counterweight to the (from his point of view exaggerated) self-conception of the *yored merkavah* with his immediate eschatology (see below).

[140] The angels.

all [types of] blows, tumours,
foul boils and wounds,
out of which damp sores seep.[141]

The Merkavah mystic has the divine approbation, "he is feared because of all his qualities and honored from those above and those below";[142] his enemies on earth, who are obviously numerous, cannot do anything against him.[143] The texts do not state who were the opponents of the Merkavah mystic; however, one can easily assume that they were likely to be found in more traditionally oriented circles. Such an immediate eschatology, as is expressed at least in the *gedullah* passages of *Hekhalot Rabbati,* only with difficulty can be reconciled with the traditional rabbinic expectation of the Messiah and the redemption.[144] Here, too, one is well advised not to render this aspect absolute—the traditional eschatology, as has been mentioned, did make its way into the manuscripts of the Hekhalot literature;[145] nevertheless, the claim of the Merkavah mystic, as ex-

---

[141]Section 84; cf. also sections 85 and 91.

[142]Section 85.

[143]This is obviously also the reason for the integration of the story of the ten martyrs in *Hekhalot Rabbati* (sections 107–121): R. Ḥananyah b. Teradyon (Neḥunyah b. Haqanah) takes the place of the Roman emperor, who is then decapitated instead of him. On the story of the ten martyrs, cf. J. Dan, "Hithawwuto u-megammotaw shel maʿaseh ʿasarah haruge malkhut," in E. Fleischer (ed.), *Studies in Literature Presented to Simon Halkin,* Jerusalem, 1973, pp. 15–22; idem., "Pirqe hekhalot u-maʿaseh ʿaseret haruge malkhut," *Eshel Beʾer Shewaʿ* 2 (1980): 63–80; G. Reeg, *Die Geschichte von den Zehn Märtyrern. Synoptische Edition mit Übersetzung und Einleitung,* Tübingen, 1985 [TSAJ 10]; there pp. 56f. on the relation of the story of the ten martyrs to the Hekhalot literature.

[144]On this point, the Hekhalot literature is closer to the eschatology of the Qumran community (cf. for example H.-W. Kuhn, *Enderwartung und gegenwärtiges Heil,* Göttingen, 1966 [STUNT 4]; H. Lichtenberger, *Studien zum Menschenbild in Texten der Qumrangemeinde,* Göttingen, 1980 [STUNT 15], pp. 218ff.) and also that of the *ḥaside ashkenaz* (see P. Schäfer, "The Ideal of Piety of the Ashkenazi Hasidim and Its Roots in Jewish Tradition," *Jewish History* 4 [1990], 9–23) than to the rabbinic literature.

[145]See above, p. 43 and n. 139. The so-called Apocalypse of David (sections 122–126) is also contained in the collections by A. Jellinek (*Bet ha-Midrash,* vol. 5, 3d ed., Jerusalem, 1967, pp. 167f.), S. Musajoff (*Merkavah Shelemah,* Jerusalem, 1921, fol. 3aff.) and Y. Even-Shemuel (*Midreshe Geʾullah,* 2d ed., Jerusalem and Tel Aviv, 1954, pp. 8ff.), the *Aggadat R. Yishmaʿel* (sections 130–138 respectively 139) under this title in Even-Shemuel (ibid., pp. 148ff.) and the Messiah Aggadah (sections 140–145) under the title *Mashiaḥ meḥayyeh metim* likewise in Even-Shemuel

emplified by the quoted texts, is of a special quality, particularly when seen in relation to the classical rabbinic Judaism.

Israel

Despite unmistakable individualistic traits in the portrayal of the Merkavah mystic (above all in the *gedullah* passages discussed earlier), the *yored merkavah* nevertheless does not stand as an individual in the center of the macroform *Hekhalot Rabbati*. On the contrary, the texts leave no doubt that the *yored merkavah* in all his peculiarity always is the representative and emissary of Israel:

Blessed unto heaven and earth
are they, who descend to the Merkavah,
when you tell and proclaim to my sons
what I do during the morning prayer,
during the Minḥah and the evening prayer,[146]
every day and at every hour,
when Israel speaks before me "holy."

Teach them and tell them:
Raise your eyes to the *raqia*ʿ
opposite your house of prayer
in the hour
when you speak before me "holy."
For I have no joy
in my entire eternal house,
which I created,
except[147] in the hour,
in which your eyes are raised to my eyes
and my eyes are raised to your eyes,
[namely] in the hour
in which you speak before me "holy."[148]

The *yored merkavah* is the emissary of Israel, whose most important task is to secure for Israel the communion with God and, as

(ibid., pp. 326f.). On the history of the transmission of these three microforms, cf. *Hekhalot-Studien*, p. 215.

[146]The evening prayer is missing in the manuscripts Munich 22, Florence 44.13 and Leiden 4730; see below, pp. 47f. and n. 163.

[147]According to the manuscripts New York 8128 and Munich 22.

[148]Section 163.

one can surely add, for God the communion with Israel. The means by which this communion is realized is the "holy, holy, holy"; that is, the *Qedushah* of the daily liturgy. During the *Qedushah,* God and Israel are closest together, and the *yored merkavah* is the witness of an intimate gesture by God, which expresses his special love for his people Israel:

> Bear witness to them[149]
> of what testimony you see in me,
> of what I do unto the face of Jacob, your father,[150]
> which is engraved [unto] me
> upon the throne of my glory.
>
> For in the hour
> when you speak before me "holy,"
> I stoop over it,
> embrace, fondle and kiss it,
> and my hands [lie] upon his arms,[151]
> three times, when you speak before me "holy,"
> as it is said:
> Holy, holy, holy [is the Lord of Hosts] [Isaiah 6:3].[152]

Now, we heard in the preceding section that the liturgy of the angels (and above all that of the *ḥayyot ha-qodesh*) culminates as well in the *Qedushah* and that a special relationship of love also exists between God and his *ḥayyot ha-qodesh;* and indeed, Israel and the *ḥayyot* find themselves in a tense and competitive relationship to one another, which in *Hekhalot Rabbati,* however, is clearly decided in Israel's favor. The texts leave no doubt that Israel's liturgy, in the end, is more important than that of the *ḥayyot*. Directly following the

---

[149]According to the manuscripts Vatican 228 and Budapest 238. The testimony of that which the *yored merkavah* sees, apparently plays an important role; cf. also sections 169 and 216. Especially noteworthy is the correspondence of sections 169 and 164: in section 169 the *yored merkavah* is supposed to give testimony to what he sees on God's countenance, in section 164 he is supposed to give testimony that God fondles Jacob's countenance. Here, the countenance of God and that of the man Jacob (as the representative of Israel) obviously are closely related to one another.

[150]According to most manuscripts.

[151]According to the manuscripts Munich 22 and Vatican 228.

[152]Section 164.

above quoted homage to the *ḥayyot* by God, in which God praises the hour in which he created the *ḥayyot,*[153] the text continues:

> Every individual angel
> and every individual Seraph,
> every individual *ḥayyah*
> and every individual Ophan,
> [which] I created,
> [should become silent],
> until I hear and heed
> the beginning of all hymns
> and praises and prayers
> and the melody of Israel's songs.[154]

As the continuation explains,[155] an individual angel with the significant name Shemaʿiʾel[156] is commissioned with the task of watching for the start of the earthly praise in the synagogues, to which the angels above then respond:

> And all ministering angels
> and all the angels [of each] individual *raqiaʿ*,
> when they[157] hear the sound of the hymns and praises,
> which Israel speaks from below,
> begin from above with: Holy, holy, holy [Isaiah 6:3].[158]

At the climax of this common earthly and heavenly *Qedushah* of the morning prayer, all of the angels, including the *ḥayyot,* cover their faces while God reveals his;[159] during the Minḥah prayer it is

---

[153]Section 173; above, p. 22.

[154]Section 174 (only in the manuscripts New York 8128 and Vatican 228).

[155]Section 178; only in the manuscripts New York 8128 and Vatican 228 (there identified as a separate tradition) and Oxford 1531 (in the context of *Seder Rabba di-Bereshit*). The unit of sections 178–188 is likely an independent tradition, which was incorporated primarily into *Seder Rabba di-Bereshit,* but also (by the redactor of MSS New York 8128 and Vatican 228) into *Hekhalot Rabbati;* cf. *Hekhalot-Studien,* pp. 267ff. The trigger undoubtedly was the end of section 173, in which the theme of the rivalry between Israel and the angels is clearly stated.

[156]The name has apparently less to do with the *Shemaʿ* but rather more with the fact that the angel "heeds" Israels prayer.

[157]According to the manuscripts Vatican 228, Oxford 1531 and Munich 22.

[158]Section 179.

[159]Sections 183f. These paragraphs belong, however, to another redactional layer

the other way around; the *ḥayyot* reveal their faces while God covers his.[160] The reason behind this alternating behavior of God appears to me to lie in the differing position of Israel. During the morning prayer the main concern is Israel's participation,[161] whereas during the Minḥah prayer, Israel is not mentioned. During the Minḥah prayer, therefore, the *ḥayyot* have, so to speak, God to themselves, they dance around him and court him and desirously long for him, but in the end, their courtship remains unsuccessful: God covers his countenance from them. Quite the contrary is the case with Israel during the morning prayer: although the angels and even the *ḥayyot* are not allowed to see God's countenance,[162] God reveals his countenance, and this can only mean to Israel. Consequently, Israel is closely connected to God during the morning prayer, God and his people see one another "from countenance to countenance"—a privilege reserved for Israel alone and not even the *ḥayyot ha-qodesh,* the bearers of the divine throne, are able to participate in it.[163] Israel is

---

than section 189 (see above, n. 155); i.e., the correspondence of the revealing and concealing of the countenance has been produced in *Hekhalot Rabbati* by the redactor of MS New York 8128. The redactor of the New York manuscript is clearly intent on intensifying the rivalrous relationship between Israel and the angels to Israel's favor.

[160]Section 189; above, p. 23.

[161]Cf. also section 296 (only in MS Budapest 238 within *Hekhalot Rabbati;* in MS New York 8128 [section 406] transmitted in the broad range of *Hekhalot Zuṭarti*), where the angels have to wait for Israel's commencement during the morning *Shemaʿ*; see *Hekhalot-Studien,* p. 266.

[162]Section 183: "so that they do not perceive the appearance of God, who resides on the Merkavah." On the rabbinic tradition that the *ḥayyot* and the ministering angels cannot see God, cf. SifBam section 103, p. 101 (ed. Horovitz) and parallels; see below, p. 57 and n. 14.

[163]The question why Israel plays no role during the Minḥah prayer is a difficult one to answer. Assuming that the main concern is the *Qedushah,* which is inserted into the repetition of the third benediction of the Tefillah, then this was, as a public communal prayer, a component of the morning, Minḥah (= afternoon) and Musaf service; as such, there exists no reason for a purely heavenly liturgy without the participation of Israel. It would be more likely, therefore, that the evening prayer is meant, in which the Qedushah is absent (as was already argued by Goldberg, "Einige Bemerkungen zu den Quellen und den redaktionellen Einheiten der Grossen Hekhalot," *FJB* 1 [1973]: 12). Arguing against this is the unanimous testimony of the Minḥah prayer in all manuscripts of section 189 and the explicit mention of the threefold "holy." We still know too little about the prayer practice that lies behind the texts of *Hekhalot Rabbati;* cf. I. Gruenwald, "Shirat ha-mal'akhim, ha-'qedushah' u-veʿayyat ḥibburah shel sifrut ha-hekhalot," in A. Oppenheimer, U. Rappaport, and M. Stern (eds.), *Jerusalem in the Second Temple Period. Abraham Schalit Memorial Volume,* Jerusalem, 1980, pp. 459–481, especially pp. 473ff; English translation in

clearly superior to the angels and also to the *ḥayyot* in both the liturgy and in the competition for God's love.

The Adjuration

It has been seen that the heavenly journey of the *yored merkavah* is immensely interspersed with magical elements. Finally, consideration must be given to a tradition in which the magic adjuration itself is the focal point. In *Hekhalot Rabbati* man is not only the *yored merkavah,* who as the emissary of Israel mediates between God and Israel, but also the subject of the magic and theurgic act of adjuration. One literary unit, which is clearly definable,[164] transforms the classical rabbinic motif of the rivalry between Israel and the angels for the Torah into the language of the Hekhalot literature (incidentally, a highly poetic language). As is the case in the Midrash, Israel longs for the Torah, and God is willing to grant his people the Torah as a pledge of their election and his particular affection toward them:

> I know what you wish,
> my heart recognizes what you desire.
> Much Torah do you wish,
> teaching in plenitude and instructions in abundance.
> You expect to ascertain Halakhah,
> you long for the fullness of my mysteries,
> in order to pile up [testimony] like mountains on mountains,
> to heap insight like hills upon hills,
> in order to make teaching great in the streets
> and Pilpul in the squares,
> to increase Halakhot like the sand of the sea
> and my mysteries like the dust of the universe;
> to found schools of learning in the gates of the tents,
> to explain prohibition and permission,
> to decree [in them] the impure for impure,

idem, *From Apocalypticism to Gnosticism,* pp. 145–173 (Gruenwald concluded from *Hekhalot Rabbati* that the *yorede merkavah* attempted to introduce to Palestine the original Babylonian usage of the *daily* recital of the *Qedushah* in the morning and Minḥah prayer); L. Renner, *Qedusha und Hekhalot,* especially pp. 70ff.

[164]Sections 281ff.; the so-called *sar ha-torah* passage (cf. *Hekhalot-Studien,* pp. 212ff.).

the pure for pure,
the declare the fit for fit,
the unfit for unfit . . . [165]

This motif of the splendor and uniqueness of the Torah, which Israel desires, is to be found in a similar form in the classical rabbinic literature;[166] surely though, an undertone already is to be heard that becomes clearer in what follows:

You[167] will rejoice,
but my servants[168] are grieved,
because this is a mystery from my mysteries
[which] leave my treasury,
from now on and [also] further.
The sound [from] your schools of learning will be [as] comforting
as [that from] the fattened calves.[169]
Not through toil and labor shall you learn,
but through the name of this seal
and through the mentioning of my crown.

The astonished is astonished by you,
and the sorrowful is sorrowful because of you.
Many die when you sigh,
their souls leave [them] when they hear of your glory.

Wealth and fortune are enormously befalling you,
the great ones of the world are attached to you.
A family, into which you marry,
is surrounded from all sides by good lineage.
He who praises with you, shall be praised,
he who extols with you, shall be extolled.
"Those who justify the many" are you called.
"Those who pronounce the creatures innocent" they call you. . . .

---

[165] Sections 287f.

[166] Cf. the corresponding texts in Schäfer, *Rivalität*, pp. 111ff.; further *Hekhalot-Studien*, pp. 269ff.

[167] Israel.

[168] The angels.

[169] Cf. Jeremiah 46:21; Malachi 3:20 and more often.

Princes will be anointed by you,
by your order, the heads of the courts stand up,
exilarchs are appointed by you,
town judges [officiate] with your permission,
for the order of the world stems from you,
and no one opposes it.[170]

The motif of the angels' opposition to the gift of the Torah is taken from rabbinic literature. New, however, is the emphasis of the absolute power promised to Israel on mastering the Torah (it recalls the power of the *yored merkavah* in the quoted *gedullah* passages) and, above all, the means by which Israel acquires the command of the Torah: no longer through toil and labor, but rather through the name of the seal and through mentioning the crown, thus, through magical means (the "great seal" and the "frightful crown" are well-known magic potencies from *Hekhalot Rabbati* and also other Hekhalot texts).[171] The opposition of the angels is directed precisely against this, as is clearly illustrated by the continuation of the text:

This mystery may not leave your treasury,
nor the secret knowledge leave your storerooms.
Do not make flesh and blood similar to us,
do not favor the children of men instead of us.
Let them toil with the Torah,
just as they toiled with the Torah
in all [previous] generations.
Let them fulfill it with exertion and great vexation.[172]

The Hekhalot literature thus goes a decisive step further than the rabbinic Midrash. The critical point is not the gift of the Torah as such, but rather the way in which Israel deals with the Torah. Whereas the rabbinic school toils with the Torah "with exertion and great vexation," the Merkavah mystic, with the help of magic aids, possesses it in a single act of perception.

Only against the background of the discussed Torah myth can one understand the numerous texts in *Hekhalot Rabbati* in which magic rituals are described that guard against forgetting the Torah. For example,

---

[170]Sections 289–291, MSS New York and Oxford.
[171]Cf. the analysis of the pertinent passages in *Hekhalot-Studien*, pp. 31ff.
[172]Section 292.

R. Yishmaʿel said:
Three years R. Neḥunyah b. Haqanah saw me
in great distress and in great agony:
A scriptural [passage], which I today read and learned,
was forgotten by me the next day.
As I saw that my study had no duration in my hand,
I raised myself, pulled myself together
[and restrained myself] from food and drink,
washing and anointment
and [abstained] from cohabitation,
and no singing or song came from my mouth. . . .

At once R. Neḥunyah b. Haqanah seized me,
took me away from the house of my father,
led me into the chamber of hewn stone
and adjured me with the great seal
[and] with the great oath. . . . [173]
When I heard this great mystery,
my eyes shone,
and everything that I heard,
[be it] Scripture, Mishnah, or something [else],
I no longer forgot.
The world was renewed [over me] in purity,
and it was as if I had come from a new world.[174]

The favored object of the adjuration is the "Prince of the Torah" (*sar ha-torah*) with whom one "binds oneself,"[175] whose "Midrash" one learns[176] and whose names one must know.[177] To such an adjuration ritual belong certain preparatory practices, as already mentioned; that is, in particular fasting and sexual abstinence, and, further, ritual baths and prayers:

He must pray this Midrash of the Prince of the Torah
three times daily after the [ʿAmidah] prayer,
so that he prays it from its beginning to its end.

---

173 There follow names (mostly *nomina barbara*).

174 Sections 308f.; cf. also sections 278f. and 677f. (*Merkavah Rabbah*). The "great mystery" is the preeminent leitmotif of *Merkavah Rabbah,* below, pp. 107ff.

175 Section 299.

176 Section 300; cf. section 298.

177 Section 298; section 313.

Thereafter he must sit down and repeat it twelve days,
days in which he must fast from morning till evening,
and he should not become silent.
At every hour when he finishes it,
he must stand upon his feet,
adjure the servants with their king,[178]
call each individual prince twelve times,[179]
and thereafter he must adjure them[180] with the seal,
[and surely] each and every one of them.[181]

There follows a long chain of names that the adept pronounces and that finally culminates in the names ʾZBWGH[182] and ṢWRTQ,[183] the names of the "great seal" and of the "frightful crown." Success of the adjuration therewith is to be guaranteed:

When he has [thus] completed twelve days,
he goes out to all the mysteries[184] of the Torah he has wished,
be it to Scripture,
be it to Mishnah,
be it to Talmud,[185]
be it to the vision of the Merkavah.[186]

The adjuration of the "Prince of the Torah" provides the adept the knowledge of the Torah in its most comprehensive sense; that is, as written and oral Torah, including the "new" discipline of the "vision of the Merkavah" propagated by the Hekhalot literature.

---

[178] That is, the angels with God. According to the manuscripts Vatican 228 and Florence Laurenziana Plut. 44.13.

[179] According to the manuscripts New York 8128, Munich 22, Vatican 228, Budapest 238, Florence 44.13 and 44.13/1.

[180] According to MS Florence 44.13.

[181] Section 300.

[182] The name consists, according to the *Atbash* method, of a combination of letters of 3 × 8 (1 + 7; 2 + 6; 3 + 5); it is possibly the Hebrew equivalent of the eighth heaven (Ogdoas) known from Gnostic sources; see Scholem, *Jewish Gnosticism*, pp. 65ff.

[183] The meaning of this name, which for the most part is mentioned together with ʾZBWGH, is unclear.

[184] According to MS Florence 44.13/1.

[185] According to the manuscripts Munich 22, Vatican 228, Budapest 238, Florence 44.13 and 44.13/1.

[186] Section 303.

3

Hekhalot Zutarti

Of all the analyzed macroforms of the Hekhalot literature, *Hekhalot Zuṭarti* is the least homogeneous. A more exact definition of the texts that constitute the macroform *Hekhalot Zuṭarti* fails due to the extreme fluidity of the manuscripts.[1] The text, on which the following observations are based,[2] therefore, with regard to the

[1]See in detail *Hekhalot-Studien*, pp. 50ff.; and *Übersetzung der Hekhalot-Literatur*, vol. 3, pp. viiff. The so-called critical edition by R. Elior (*Hekhalot Zuṭarti. Mahadurah mada*ʿ*it*, Jerusalem, 1982 [JSJT, Suppl. 1] does not in any way do justice to the particularity of the text; see D. J. Halperin, "A New Edition of the Hekhalot Literature," *JAOS* 104 (1984): 546ff.; P. Schäfer, "Mahadurah biqortit shel Hekhalot Zuṭarti," *Tarbiz* 54 (1984): 153–157.

[2]Essentially sections 335–374 and 407–426; whereby these two sections, later, as shall be seen, display substantial differences, both formally and with regards to their contents.

"identity establishing" function of the macroform, is more arbitrary than the other macroforms.

God

The Power of the Divine Name

In *Hekhalot Zuṭarti,* the omnipotent strength of the divine name[3] is a much more dominant theme than in *Hekhalot Rabbati.* If it is at all possible to denominate a focal point in *Hekhalot Zuṭarti,* it is the name of God, around which the thoughts of the authors or redactors revolve. On his ascent to God, Moses perceived the names that guard against forgetting the Torah;[4] the "name" likewise was revealed to ʿAqiva so that it could be passed on to his students:

> A [great] name is he,
> a holy name is he,
> a pure name is he.
> Because each one, who makes use [of it]
> in fright, in fear, in purity,
> in holiness, in humility,
> the seeds will be multiplied
> and shall be successful in all his endeavors,
> and his days shall be long.[5]

The name of God works wonders—with it, Moses was able to part the sea and pile the waters up into high "mountains"[6]—and it is of cosmic potency.[7] It is self-evident that not only one name is meant, but rather multiple variations and permutations, for the most part unintelligible *nomina barbara,*[8] several of which are likely of Greek origin.[9] God's mysterious essence consists of names, whose various forms have been handed down by Balaam, Moses, the angel

---

[3]Section 365; *shem shel gevurah,* "name of strength."
[4]Sections 336, 340.
[5]Section 337 = 347.
[6]Sections 342f.
[7]Sections 348, 367.
[8]Section 351.
[9]Cf. section 357: "This is the *shem ha-meforash* [= the inexplicable name of God], its explanation, its investigation and its pronunciation; and its explanation is Greek."

of death, David, and Solomon.[10] In sections 362f., ʿAqiva transmits a long chain of names (a combination of *nomina barbara* and intelligible epithets), which are transformed into (in part) identifiable names of angels and then culminate in names of God (*shaddai, qadosh, ehye asher ehye*).[11] Here, too, the observation is confirmed that the names of God and those of the angels are used interchangeably and that they cannot always be clearly separated.[12]

Can One See God?

Hekhalot Zuṭarti is the only text in the Hekhalot literature that directly asks the question whether one can see God. Although God's "beauty" (*yofi*), which the Merkavah mystic "sees"[13] also is referred to here, in the ascension reports of sections 407ff. (influenced by *Hekhalot Rabbati?*), these formulations nevertheless give the impression of being standard, adopted expressions; on the other hand, the question whether one can see God at all, and if yes, then who, and what he looks like is posed in a poignant manner not encountered before:[14]

> Who is able to explain, who is able to see?
> Firstly, it is written [Exodus 33:20]: For man may not see me and live.
> And secondly, it is written [Deuteronomy 5:21–24]: That man may live though God has spoken to him.

---

[10]Sections 357ff.

[11]The sections 362–365 also are elements of the *Havdalah de-Rabbi ʿAqiva* (ed. Scholem, *Tarbiz* 50 [1980–81]: 243–281; cf. also *Synopse,* p. xi; *Geniza-Fragmente zur Hekhalot-Literatur,* p. 152; *Übersetzung der Hekhalot-Literatur,* vol. 3, pp. 43ff.

[12]Cf. K.-E. Grözinger, "Die Namen Gottes und der himmlischen Mächte—Ihre Funktion und Bedeutung in der *Hekhalot*-Literatur," *FJB* 13 (1985): especially pp. 38ff.

[13]Characteristic of sections 335–374 appears to be the "glory" (*kavod*); cf. sections 335 and 346 (in section 335, however, the phrase *beauty of the Merkavah* likewise is to be found).

[14]Cf. the rabbinical texts on the vision of the Shekhinah, which in part also revolve around Exodus 33:20 (Sifra to Leviticus 1:1, p. 18 [ed. Finkelstein, vol. 2]; SifBam section 103, p. 101 [ed. Horovitz]; TanBuber *bamidbar* section 20; PRE ch. 32, fol. 73b [ed. Warsaw 1851–52]; ShemR 3, 1; PRE ch. 46, fol. 111bf.), and to the whole Goldberg, *Schekhinah,* pp. 257ff, 513ff.; Schäfer, *Rivalität,* pp. 207ff.

> And thirdly, it is written [Isaiah 6:1]: I beheld my Lord seated upon a high and lofty throne.[15]

This text does not answer the question in an abstract-theoretical way, but through the simple contrast of biblical verses. There can be no doubt that the answer lies in the ordering of the verses: Exodus 33:20 and Deuteronomy 5:21–24 form, so to speak, the thesis (man cannot see God and remain alive) and the antithesis (man can speak with God and remain alive), whereas Isaiah 6:1 offers the solution. The visionary (Isaiah = the *yored merkavah*) sees God on his throne in the seventh *hekhal* and sustains no injury. It is surely no mere coincidence that directly following the quotation from Isaiah,[16] no description of God's appearance on the throne is provided, but rather the question "and what is his name?" is posed. This entails that the name of God is the crucial revelation for the Merkavah mystic. The connection to the preceding passage is made clear by the fact that, following the lists of names, the quotation from Isaiah 6:1 is expressly repeated. The "vision" of God consists, so to speak, of the communication of his names.

The next section then explicitly poses the question, with a further intensification, concerning God's appearance.[17] The angels see him like "something that looked like flares,"[18] the prophets in a dream[19] in a vision of the night;[20] the manner in which the kings of the earth see him in all manuscripts is either unintelligible[21] or corrupt. Then come R. ʿAqiva and Moses:

> But R. [ʿAqiva] said:
> He is, so to say, as we are,
> but he is greater than everything
> and his glory consists in this,
> that he is concealed from us.[22]

---

[15]Section 350.

[16]Section 351.

[17]Section 352.

[18]Cf. Ezekiel 1:14.

[19]Cf. Job 33:15.

[20]Cf. Isaiah 29:7; Daniel 8:1 and more often.

[21]Greek?

[22]Or, "And therein [that he is greater] consists his glory that is concealed from us."

Moses said to them, to these ones and those ones:
Do not investigate your words,[23]
instead he should be praised at his place.
Therefore, it is said [Ezekiel 3:12]:
Blessed be the glory of the Lord in his place.[24]

Here as well, the gist lies undoubtedly in the order of the statements. The angels see (and know) the least; there follow the prophets, the kings of earth and ʿAqiva. ʿAqiva's description is the climax of the *positive* possible statements about God: he looks like us, like man, although he is of tremendous dimensions and—therein the positive statement is immediately restrained—in the end concealed from us. The fact remains, however, that ʿAqiva (and *only* ʿAqiva) can transmit the knowledge that God "so to speak" (*kiv-yakhol*) looks like a man.

The concluding dictum of Moses is no longer a positive statement concerning God's appearance, respectively the question whether man can see him, but instead forms the anticlimax to the previous list culminating in ʿAqiva's dictum: decisive is not what God looks like, but that he is praised "at his place"; that is, wherever he is and in whatever way he can be described. The task of the angels and that of man is to praise God during the daily liturgy. This is surely the traditional and, for all Hekhalot texts, conclusive statement; nevertheless, with ʿAqiva's dictum the text dared, as hardly another, to enter into areas otherwise avoided (that the author or redactor was conscious of the risk of his statement is supported by the *kiv-yakhol*). *Hekhalot Zuṭarti* thereby appears, despite the ambivalence on the question of whether one can see God and what he looks like,[25] to take a clear stand: God revealed himself to ʿAqiva as the prototype of the *yored merkavah,* and ʿAqiva is authorized to transmit this revelation to man:

The great, mighty and frightful, grand and powerful God,
who is hidden from the eyes of all creatures
and concealed from the ministering angels,

---

[23]Cf. also section 335 ("do not investigate the words of your lips").

[24]Section 352.

[25]Cf. also section 356: "which no being can perceive, and his body is like beryl [Daniel 10:6] [and] fills the whole world, so that [those] close and [those] far [can] not observe [him]."

but revealed to R. ʿAqiva through the work of the Merkavah in order to fulfill his wish.[26]

Shiʿur Qomah

In connection with ʿAqiva's dictum of the human appearance of God, one would expect in *Hekhalot Zuṭarti* especially, a distinct tendency toward *Shiʿur Qomah* speculations, however, exactly this is not the case; in contrast to Scholem's statement, *Shiʿur Qomah* speculations are decidedly rare in *Hekhalot Zuṭarti.*[27] The only direct indication of the incorporation of *Shiʿur Qomah* traditions in *Hekhalot Zuṭarti* is to be found in the extensive quotation from the Song of Songs verses (5:10–16) in section 419, which goes on to the names of God and concludes with the trishagion from Isaiah 6:3. These verses are justly associated with *Shiʿur Qomah* speculations,[28] though absent here is any reference to the measurements and names of God's limbs that otherwise is characteristic of the *Shiʿur Qomah* speculations.[29]

God as King

Paragraphs 407–426 of *Hekhalot Zuṭarti*[30] are to be clearly differentiated from the previously considered sections 335–374 in regard to both form and content and display numerous similarities with *Hekhalot Rabbati.* Therefore, it is not very surprising that here the same theology of the king with which we are familiar from *He-*

---

[26]Section 421. The passage thereby belongs to the second section of *Hekhalot Zuṭarti* = sections 407–426, which in form and content is clearly discernible from the first; see below, n. 30.

[27]Scholem, *Jewish Gnosticism,* p. 76: "most of the book's content is devoted to descriptions not to be found in the Greater Hekhalot, and especially to theurgical instructions of considerable age and to fragments of the *Shiʿur Komah* teaching." Scholem concretely bases this last statement on sections 352 (cf. p. 79) and 367; however, neither is a *Shiʿur Qomah* text in the true sense.

[28]Cf. above all the Appendix D by S. Lieberman in Scholem's *Jewish Gnosticism,* pp. 118ff.

[29]Cf. sections 688ff. in the macroform *Merkavah Rabbah* (see below, pp. 99ff. and *Hekhalot-Studien,* p. 28; Cohen, *The Shiʿur Qomah: Texts and Recensions,* pp. 54ff; K. Herrmann, "Text und Fiktion. Zur Textüberlieferung des *Shiʿur Qoma,*" *FJB* 16 [1988]: 89–142) and, outside these borders of the macroform *Hekhalot Zuṭarti,* extensively also sections 480–488 in MS Munich 22.

[30]Within this unit, sections 420–424 once again are to be differentiated; see below, pp. 65f.

khalot Rabbati is dominant; the names of God play next to no role. We find the well-known formula from *Hekhalot Rabbati* "to behold the king in his beauty"[31] and, as in *Hekhalot Rabbati,* litanies of the king.[32] At the climax of his ascent, the *yored merkavah* praises God as the omnipotent king:

> King, seated upon a high and exalted throne . . .
> He sees into the depths,
> gazes into that which is concealed,
> looks into darkness.
> At every place, you are there,
> in every heart do you rest,
> your wish cannot be changed [by anyone],
> your word not answered,
> your will not delayed; . . .
> Lord over all actions,
> wise in all mysteries,
> ruler in every generation,
> [the] one God, who has always been,
> sole king, who is for ever and ever. Sela.
> Ruler over those above and those below,
> over the first, over the last. . . .
> Those above and those below kneel and prostrate themselves before you, Lord, God of Israel.
> Seraphim glorify and rejoice before you, Lord, God of Israel.
> The throne of your glory praises and gives you pride and dignity,
> strength and splendor before you, Lord, God of Israel.
> Your servants crown you with crowns and sing a new song to you.
> They install you as king forever,
> and you shall be called One forever and ever.[33]

This text intersects in manifold ways with *Hekhalot Rabbati*[34] and more likely is influenced by *Hekhalot Rabbati* than the other way around. The central importance of the idea of God's royal power in the context of the ascent traditions is confirmed.

[31]Sections 407–409, 411, 412.

[32]Section 412.

[33]Section 418.

[34]Cf. sections 256 = 265; 257 = 266; 274; 276; cf. also section 162 (the hymn of the throne), above, pp. 13f.

Angels

The angels play a notably minor roll in *Hekhalot Zuṭarti;* the text is remote from any attempt at a reflected, let alone systematic, angelology. Their otherwise so dominant function as the princely household responsible for the divine liturgy and as bearers of the divine throne appears for the most part to be irrelevant.

The *ḥayyot ha-qodesh*

In the textual unit of sections 335–374, essentially only the *ḥayyot ha-qodesh* are mentioned. They are apparently so closely connected to God, that man can infer from their appearance the appearance of God. Following the passage that treats God's appearance,[35] the text continues:

> Anyone who wants to learn this secret,[36]
> shall learn knowledge from the *ḥayyot,*
> who are before him:
> [from] their gait,
> from their appearance,
> [from] their faces,
> [from] their wings.
> Their gait is like the appearance [of the lightning],
> their appearance is like the appearance of the rainbow in the cloud,
> their faces are like the appearance of the bride,[37]
> their wings are like the radiance of the clouds of glory.[38]

Thereafter, the exact number of the faces and wings of the *ḥayyot* is calculated[39] and the way they move with their 4 × 4 (= 16)

---

[35]Section 352; above, pp. 57ff.

[36]What is meant is obviously the secret of the (human) appearance of God.

[37]*De-kalla?* On the metaphor of bride and groom, cf. for example sections 94; 154; 420 (the Genizah fragment T.-S. K 21.95.C, fol. 2b, l. 44 = *Geniza-Fragmente zur Hekhalot-Literatur,* p. 105, and *Übersetzung der Hekhalot-Literatur,* vol. 3, p. 178); 687.

[38]Section 353. The text obviously is influenced by the description of the *ḥayyot* in Ezekiel 1:5ff.

[39]Section 354.

respectively $4 \times 4 \times 4$ ($= 64$) faces and wings[40] is described. The text is more or less corrupt in all manuscripts and is reproduced here on the basis of a Genizah fragment:[41]

When they want to gaze,
they gaze behind them toward the west.
When they want to look,
they look [at that which is] in front of them, toward the east.

When they go,
they go with the outer
and turn around with the inner [wings].

When they turn around,
they turn around with the inner
and cover their bodies with the [outer[42] wings].

When they pray,
they pray with the outer
and fall silent with the inner [wings].

When they go,
they rage and shake the world
through their gait,
through their appearance,
through their faces,
and through their wings.

The next section[43] to some degree describes the heavenly geography in the area between the soles of the feet of the *ḥayyot* and God on the throne of his glory: between the *ḥayyot* and the divine throne (likewise based on the Genizah fragment) are found hailstones, stones of broom fire, beryl stones, clouds of consolation, rows of saints (= angels), spirits and *Lilin,*[44] rivers of fire, and finally one reaches the area that according to the verse Job 26:9 is

---

[40]Cf. Targum Ezekiel 1:6.

[41]T.-S. K 21.95.B, fol. 2b, lines 4–8 = *Geniza-Fragmente zur Hekhalot-Literatur,* p. 89.

[42]The "inner" here in the text is corrupt.

[43]Section 356.

[44]Demons of the night; cf. for example Targum Ps–Jon Numbers 6:24; Deuteronomy 32, 24; T.-S. K 1.30, 1. 5 (quoted in: P. Schäfer, "Jewish Magic Literature in Late Antiquity and Early Middle Ages," *JJS* 41 [1990]: 84f.).

called *meʾaḥez pene kisse* ("he shuts off the view of His throne") and *parshez ʿalaw ʿanano* ("spreading over it His clouds")—in other words, one finds oneself so close to the throne that one can touch it (a play on words, *oḥez,* "he grasps"/*meʾaḥez,* "he shuts off")—whereby the throne itself (and the figure seated on it) is enshrouded by a cloud. The previously quoted statement that one can infer from the appearance of the *ḥayyot* the appearance of God thereby is relativized. As close as the *ḥayyot* are to God, so far are they from him at the same time; as overwhelming and radiant as their appearance is to the observer, so incomparable and in the end concealed, even for one who comes very close, is the appearance of God on the throne.[45] Here once again, the paradox of the simultaneously hidden and revealed God is clearly displayed; God who can be seen neither by the angels nor by man and who, nonetheless, revealed his secret to R. ʿAqiva and thus to the *yored merkavah.*

The *ḥayyot* and the Throne

Within the textual unit of sections 335–374, the sections 368–374 constitute a particular unit, which can be assumed as having not originally belonged to the Hekhalot texts. Either it was inserted here by the *ḥaside ashkenaz,* or an original piece from the Hekhalot literature was thoroughly revised by them.[46] Here, further details concerning the *ḥayyot* and the throne are communicated: the names of the four feet of the throne and their respectively appointed *ḥayyot;*[47] the appearance of the *ḥayyot* with their human, lion, bull, and eagle faces;[48] the way in which they move;[49] the appearance of the throne;[50] the curtain in front of the divine throne with the angels in front and behind it;[51] the throne, the *ḥayyot,* and the Ophannim;[52] the letters opposite the crown.[53] In total, we are dealing with a compilation of various traditions and comments on them, which does not provide any essentially new insights.

---

[45]Cf. also Targum Ezekiel 1:27.

[46]On the Ashkenazi redaction of the Hekhalot literature, see above, p. 6, n. 15.

[47]Section 368.

[48]Section 369.

[49]Section 370.

[50]Section 371; cf. b Soṭ 17a.

[51]Section 372; cf. PRE ch. 4, fol. 9bf. (ed. Warsaw 1851–52). On the curtain in front of God's throne, cf. also sections 346 and 64f. (3 Enoch), below, p. 135 and n. 70.

[52]Section 373.

[53]Section 374. Cf. also sections 633 (the letters engraved on the crown); 636 (the

Guardians and Examiners; Individual Angels

The second large textual unit in the macroform *Hekhalot Zuṭarti,*[54] with regard to its concept of the angels, also clearly is separate from the unit of sections 335–374. As was the case with the conception of God, this section in particular apparently is influenced by *Hekhalot Rabbati*. This is true first of all of the function of the angels as examiners of the adept at the entrance to the sixth *hekhal*[55] and applies in general to their capacity as guardian angels at the entrances to all six respectively seven *hekhalot;*[56] it is displayed furthermore by the emphasis of a number of angelic princes, with whom we are acquainted from *Hekhalot Rabbati* (and naturally from other macroforms).

A whole section[57] is devoted to a mysterious angel who is named by God alone as MGHShH.[58] Insofar as he is expressly referred to as "the second [in rank]" after God himself and as his name is "one" with the divine name, we can only be dealing with Meṭaṭron.[59] He prepares the throne for the descent of God, dresses God[60] with his special garment (the *ḥaluq,* "shirtlike robe"),[61] adorns the *ḥashmal,* and opens the gates of redemption.[62] This function of Meṭaṭron may be related to that of the angel of the countenance in *Hekhalot Rabbati,* who arranges the throne of glory and prepares the "seat for the noble of Jacob."[63]

ʿAnafiʾel, who likewise is known from *Hekhalot Rabbati,*[64] appears here in a connection most difficult to interpret. According to

---

letters which "hover above the throne of glory"); 16 (the letters on Meṭaṭron's crown that "fly on high"); 57 (the letters engraved on the throne of glory that "fly like eagles with sixteen wings").

[54]Sections 407–426.

[55]Sections 407ff.: the sixth *hekhal* obviously is the location of the last test before the entrance to the seventh *hekhal,* in which the throne of glory stands; see also above, p. 38 (*Hekhalot Rabbati*).

[56]Sections 413ff.; see below, p. 74.

[57]Section 420.

[58]With variations; cf. *Übersetzung der Hekhalot-Literatur,* vol. 3, p. 175.

[59]In the Genizah fragment T.-S. K 21.95.C, fol. 2b, l. 42f. (= *Geniza-Fragmente zur Hekhalot-Literatur,* p. 105), he is referred to as "faithful servant" (*mesharet neʾeman*), "for my name and his name are one." Cf. also *Übersetzung zur Hekhalot-Literatur,* vol. 3, p. 177.

[60]And not the *kavod,* as Scholem argues, *Jewish Gnosticism,* p. 63.

[61]See above, pp. 18f.

[62]Section 420.

[63]Section 170; above, p. 29.

[64] See above, pp. 30f.

the classical Hekhalot manuscripts,[65] he acts as the protector of one who "desires to gain insight into the work of his creator [= God]"[66] and fulfills his wishes; the opponent of the Merkavah mystic, who spreads "evil rumors" about him,[67] is beaten and destroyed by him. This unequivocal statement is reversed by the Genizah fragment in exactly the opposite, as it has ʿAnafiʾel threatening one who attempts to adjure him with precisely this punishment.[68] Whereas in the manuscripts of the *Synopse* it thus is the opponents of the Merkavah mystics who are criticized, in the Geniza fragment it is the Merkavah mystics themselves. It is true that the relation between the two versions can be hardly more exactly determined, however, the completely opposing tendency is remarkable enough. Here for the first time in a Hekhalot text do we find implicit criticism of the practice of adjuration by the Hekhalot mystic; why this is connected precisely with the angelic prince ʿAnafiʾel remains obscure.[69]

Finally, the two concluding paragraphs of the textual unit of sections 407–426 also mention the "Prince of the Countenance," Suriya, who, in a manner similar to *Hekhalot Rabbati*[70] and with the same introductory formula, functions as R. Yishmaʿel's angel of revelation; the question whether these sections belong to the macroform *Hekhalot Zutarti,* as may be expected, is controversial.[71]

Man

In *Hekhalot Zuṭarti* as well, the ascent of the *yored merkavah* is the central point of interest, albeit in a very specific manner and with varying importance in the respective textual units.

---

[65]Section 421.

[66]*Maʿaseh yoṣro* evidently alludes to the *yoṣer bereshit* of section 244 in *Hekhalot Rabbati;* see above, p. 31 and n. 83.

[67]The same phrase as in the *gedullah* passages, section 84; see above, p. 43.

[68]T.-S. K 21.95.C, fol. 2b, 1.45ff. = *Geniza-Fragmente zur Hekhalot-Literatur,* p. 105; and *Übersetzung der Hekhalot-Literatur,* vol. 3, pp. 179f.: "Each one who names me one of the names of [my] four servants and at once therewith adjures me—[so] do I turn neither forward nor backwards, neither to the right nor to the left, before I at once strike and [dispel] him and drag him on his face, . . . at once do I strike him, destroy him and no longer grant him a delay."

[69]In the Genizah fragment the text is referred to at the end as *gevurat ʿAnafiʾel.*

[70]Sections 117ff.; 152.

[71]Despite the general problems concerning the delimitation of this macroform; see above, p. 55 and n. 1 and 2.

The Ascent of Moses and ʿAqiva

In the textual unit defined by sections 335–374 the main concern is strikingly (and quite contrary to *Hekhalot Rabbati,* for example) not the ascent of the *yored merkavah* proper, but the ascent of Moses and R. ʿAqiva. Moses and ʿAqiva obviously function as the prototypes of the Merkavah mystic and possibly as heroes of the past as well (Moses as the role model for ʿAqiva and ʿAqiva as role model for the *yored merkavah*).[72] At the very beginning, we read the following concerning Moses' ascent:

> When Moses ascended on high to God, the Holy One, blessed be he, taught him:
> Anyone, whose heart goes astray,[73]
> recite over him these names, in the name of . . . ,[74]
> so that everything that I see and hear will be grasped by my heart,
> [namely] Bible, Mishnah, Talmud, Halakhot, and Haggadot,
> so that I will never forget,
> [not] in this world and not in the world to come.[75]

Here already, the central topic is apparent: the ascent (of Moses) communicates the knowledge of the divine names that guard against forgetting the Torah. The ascent, therefore, is closely connected to the adjuration, it has a theurgic function.

---

[72]The only passage within the sections 335–374 in which the ascent and power of the *yored merkavah* in general is referred to is section 349 (duplicate section 361): "What is the man that he is able to ascend upwards, to ride [on the] wheels, to descend downwards, to explore the world, to walk on dry land, to behold his radiance, . . . [?] his crown, to be transformed through his honor, to say praise, to combine signs, to say names, to peer upwards and to peer downwards, to know exactly the living and to behold the vision of the dead, to walk in rivers of fire and to know the lightning." This, however, certainly is not independent ascent tradition, but embedded in the ʿAqiva traditions and in the question whether man can see God at all.

[73]According to the manuscripts New York 8128, Munich 22, and Dropsie 436.

[74]There follow a number of mostly unintelligible *nomina barbara*.

[75]Section 336; cf. section 340: "You, these holy names, open my heart. Everything that I hear, be it the words of the Torah, be it all the words of the world, they should be preserved in my heart, and nothing should be forgotten by me."

The same is undoubtedly true of ʿAqiva's ascent. As the story of the four rabbis who entered the *pardes,* which is inserted at two places, desires to show,[76] ʿAqiva is the only one who survived the ascent unharmed and who thus was authorized to transmit the mysteries he had seen and heard. Ben ʿAzzai died, Ben Zoma went mad, Elishaʿ b. Avuyah (= Aḥer) spread heresy; only ʿAqiva "entered unharmed and left unharmed";[77] to him alone can the verse Song of Songs 1:4 be applied: "Draw me after you, let us run! The king has brought me to his chambers." It is true that the *pardes* story itself does not mention the concrete purpose of ʿAqiva's successfully undertaken ascent—it very likely was taken by the redactor from an earlier source and intentionally incorporated here. However, its placement within the context of the surrounding blocks of text clearly illustrates what the redactor intended to state. Directly before the first version of the *pardes* story and in duplicate directly following the second version we read:

> This is the name, which was revealed to R. ʿAqiva
> when he observed the working of the Merkavah.
> ʿAqiva [again] descended[78] and taught it to his students.
> He said to them:
> My sons, handle this name carefully,
> [for] it is a [great] name,
> it is a holy name,
> it is a pure name.
> Because each one, who makes use of it in fright, in fear,
> in purity, in holiness, in humility,
> will multiply the seeds,
> be successful in all his endeavors,
> and his days shall be long.[79]

The result of ʿAqiva's "vision of the Merkavah" is the knowledge of the divine name and its transmission to his students. Although here the result of the knowledge and use of the name is "only" numerous descendants and a long life, the theurgic potency of the name nevertheless is beyond all doubt. God established the

---

[76]Sections 338f. and 344f.

[77]Section 344.

[78]Cf. to the terminology above, p. 2, n. 4.

[79]Section 337; cf. also section 347.

"firm name in order to plan the whole world with it."[80] Following a long list of names is the hymnic description of the cosmic potency transmitted through the names:

> This is the oath and the seal,
> with which one binds the earth
> and with which one binds the heavens.
> The earth flees from it
> and the universe shudders in front of it.
> It opens the mouth of the sea
> and closes the hooks of the firmament;
> it opens the heavens
> and floods[81] the universe.
> It uproots the earth
> and whirls the universe into confusion—QShTʾ RWMʾ QWSTYNʾ is its name,
> HWRBʾ MSMSYYʾ is its name.[82]

The knowledge of the divine name, therefore, also can be transposed in a concrete adjuration:

> Blessed be his name,
> the great, frightful, mighty,
> daring, powerful and noble,
> which our eyes desire
> and with which we adjure:
> I adjure you, MQLYTW, with the name. . . . [83]

The Danger of the Divine Name

Closely connected to the theurgic potency of the divine name is the frequent emphasis on the danger of the name and the admonition to handle it carefully. Whereas the ascent was reserved for Moses and ʿAqiva, the name is accessible to ʿAqiva's students and therewith to a circle of "initiates." This is the theme of the section

[80]Or "to strengthen"; section 348.
[81]"Makes drunk"?
[82]Section 367.
[83]There follows once again a long list of unintelligible *nomina barbara;* section 357.

generally taken to be the introductory paragraph of the macroform *Hekhalot Zuṭarti:*

> If you want to be singled out[84] in the world
> so that the secrets of the world and the mysteries of wisdom should be revealed to you,
> study this Mishnah and be careful about it
> till the day of your passing.[85]
> Do not try to understand what lies behind you[86]
> and do investigate the words of your lips.
> You should try to understand what is in your heart and keep silent,
> so that you will be worthy of the beauty of the Merkavah.
> Be careful about the glory of your creator
> and do not descend to it.[87]
> When you [however] have descended to it, do not enjoy anything of it.
> Your end would then be to be banished from the world.
> The glory of God [is]:
> Conceal the matter,[88] so that you will not be banished from the world.[89]

This text is a purposeful revision of given Rabbinic motifs. The well-known prohibition from m Ḥagiga 2:1 of *Maʿaseh Bereshit* and *Maʿaseh Merkavah* is taken up in a quite playful manner and used for the Merkavah mysticism.[90] The "chosen" adept, ʿAqiva's

[84]Among the other men; see below, n. 90.

[85]Perhaps also "your separation" in the sense of mystical-ascetic practices.

[86]Or also in a temporal sense: "what comes after you"; cf. m Ḥag 2, 1.

[87]The glory. The "reversed" terminology of the descent to the Merkavah is again to be noted here; see above, p. 68 and p. 2, n. 4.

[88]This is an interpretation of the biblical verse Proverbs 25:2. The Masoretic text ("It is the glory of God to conceal a matter") is reinterpreted: when you have "experienced" the glory of God during your descent to the Merkavah, do not make it public, for it is not destined for everyone.

[89]Section 335.

[90]It is even possible that the beginning of section 335 (*im attah roṣeh le-hityaḥed,* literally, "if you wish to be isolated and unique"), intentionally refers to m Ḥag 2:1: "One does not expound the Merkavah to one [*be-yaḥid*], unless he is wise and understands of his own knowledge." The meaning of the beginning of *Hekhalot Zuṭarti* then would be: if you wish to be the *one,* to whom the Merkavah, as an exception, can be expounded, learn this Mishnah, etc.

student, who belongs to the circle of "initiates," is allowed to learn "this Mishnah"—thereby, of course, the Mishnah in Ḥagiga 2:1 is not meant, but rather the "Mishnah" of the Merkavah mystic—if only he handles it in the correct, that is careful, manner. We find ourselves here within a *closed group* who transmits its knowledge only within the group and not outside of it; and this knowledge is clearly to be understood as secret, and thus *esoteric,* knowledge. The theurgic potency connected with the knowledge of the divine name is intended only for those who belong to this group—who belongs to it (and based on what criteria) is something we do not learn; we know only that the members of this group consider themselves " ʿAqiva's students."

In a similarly artistic manner, given motifs from rabbinic literature are adapted in another text:

> He used to say:
> Who spreads [his] name, loses his name
> and who does not learn, deserves death.
> Who makes use of the crown, vanishes.
> Who does not know QYNTMYSʾ, shall be put to death,
> and who knows QYNTMYSʾ, will be desired in the world to come.[91]

It is not difficult to recognize in this passage Hillel's famous dictum from m Avot 1:13[92] that, however, is given a fully new meaning. "He" is no longer Hillel but ʿAqiva, and the name that is "spread" is no longer the name of the (ambitious) man but rather the name of God. In the new context of the Merkavah mysticism, the concern likewise is the warning against the further transmission of esoteric knowledge. Here, the making use of the crown very likely no longer denotes, as Scholem already suggested,[93] the "crown of the Torah" in Hillel's dictum, but rather the improper and careless use of the secret name of God. Only the mysterious QYNTMYSʾ is without parallel in Hillel's dictum; however, it is quite certain that

---

[91] Section 360.

[92] "One who makes his name great, loses his name; one who does not add, perishes. One who does not learn, is liable to death; one who makes use of the crown, passes away."

[93] *Jewish Gnosticism*, pp. 80 and 54.

it is also to be understood in a magical sense:[94] the true mystic, the one who belongs to the circle of initiates, knows QYNTMYSʾ and thus is destined for the world to come (i.e., the future life).

The Book of Merkavah Mysticism

The Merkavah mysticism in *Hekhalot Zuṭarti* finally, as a secret teaching for a select few, is an esoteric *discipline*. This follows from the emphasis on learning[95] and the explicit allusion that the secret teaching of Moses was revealed in a book:

> This is the book of wisdom, understanding, and perception,
> the investigation of things above and things below,
> the hidden things of the Torah,
> of heaven and of earth,
> and the secrets, which were given to Moses, son of ʿAmram
> of the perception of YH YH ʾHYH Yʾ W ṢBʾ WT,
> the God of Israel . . . [96]

Here, the transition from an (ecstatic?) practice to a literary form of Merkavah mysticism seems to be accomplished. The initiate learns the secrets of his esoteric discipline (without doubt the correct names) from a book, which has found its way from Moses to ʿAqiva and then to him as a member of a group of chosen ones. To what extent this emphasis on the literary character of Merkavah mysticism is valid for the entire macroform *Hekhalot Zuṭarti* is hard to judge.[97] True, the above quoted text is transmitted only in MS New York; nonetheless, the emphasis on learning also is to be found in the unit of sections 407–426 (sections 419; 424),[98] and the last sec-

---

[94]Regardless of the meaning of the word. Scholem, *Jewish Gnosticism*, pp. 80f., following Lieberman, wishes to derive it from *kainotomein*, "to introduce something new."

[95]Cf. sections 335 and 336 = 340.

[96]Section 341 (only in MS New York 8128).

[97]Whereby the various layers within the macroform must be taken into account. Cf. also the unit of sections 489–495, which in some manuscripts is ascribed to the macroform *Hekhalot Rabbati* (see *Hekhalot-Studien*, pp. 207f., 212), in which the book also plays a central role. The notion of the book probably belongs more in a magical context, rather than in that of the Merkavah (heavenly journey); however, these two tendencies are closely connected exactly in *Hekhalot Zuṭarti*.

[98]Section 419: "Learn this Mishnah every day after prayer"; section 424: "Everyone who wishes to learn this Mishnah and to explain the name."

tion considered part of the macroform *Hekhalot Zuṭarti* once again refers explicitly to the book. One therefore can assume, at least in regard to the final redactor, that for him a literary stage of Merkavah mysticism was decisive:

> Everyone who deals carefully with this book and purifies himself,
> he is loved by [the] angels, *er'elim,* troops, Seraphim, Keruvim, Ophannim and [the] throne of glory.
> The righteous, the honest and the fathers of the world pray for his vitality,
> and give him possession of the Gan Eden.[99]

Ascent and Adjuration

The unit of sections 407–426 likewise stresses the special role of ʿAqiva as prototype of the Merkavah mystic,[100] but in contrast to sections 335–374, deals essentially with the ascent of the *yored merkavah* proper, his examination,[101] and his success (the vision of the king "in his beauty"); as mentioned earlier,[102] this section likely is influenced by *Hekhalot Rabbati.* Even the very central motif in *Hekhalot Rabbati* of God's love for Israel is found in this connection in *Hekhalot Zuṭarti:*

> Just like the light of the countenance of Jacob, our father,
> will shine before 'DYRYRWN, the Lord, the God of Israel,
> our father, who is in heaven . . . ,
> [so] does the love of the beloved people come closer
> to HDYRYRWN, the Lord, the God of Israel,
> our father, who is in heaven,
> beneath clouds and denseness that drip blood.[103]

The worthy *yored merkavah* is received in the seventh *hekhal* amiably by the angels and may take a seat in front of the throne of glory:

---

99 Section 426.
100 Cf. sections 422f.
101 Sections 407f., 409f.
102 Above, pp. 63f.
103 Section 411; cf. section 215 = *Hekhalot Rabbati.*

> Everyone who is worthy to see the king in his beauty,
> enter and see.
> If it is so,
> the Ophannim of might embrace him,
> the Keruvim of majesty kiss him,
> the *ḥayyot* carry him,
> the morning star dances before him,
> Ḥashma' el sings before him,[104]
> the lively wind of brightness bears him,
> until they raise him up
> and set him down before the throne of glory.[105]

A second unit of ascent traditions provides, likewise in the same manner as *Hekhalot Rabbati,* a detailed instruction of the ascent (in the second person singular) with the names and seals of the guardian angels at the entrances to the seven *hekhalot.*[106] Having reached the goal of his desires, the adept is seated on God's lap and called upon to state his request.[107] Characteristically, the *yored merkavah* begins his request with a long song of praise of God as king, only at the end of which is stated his actual request:

> Let me find grace and favor before the throne of glory
> and in the eyes of all your servants,
> and bind unto me all your servants,
> to do this and that.[108]

Here, in stark contrast to *Hekhalot Rabbati,* the ascent is connected to the adjuration, and the ascent of the *yored merkavah* receives a theurgic meaning atypical of *Hekhalot Rabbati,* but very

---

[104]The name of the angel alludes to the *ḥashmal* ("gleam as of amber") of Ezekiel 1:4.27; cf. also section 407.

[105]Ibid. The fact that the *yored merkavah* is allowed to sit before God undoubtedly contains a polemical gist against the background of b Ḥag 15a (Aḥer finds Meṭaṭron seated in heaven, concludes from this "two deities" and thereby causes Meṭaṭron's punishment).

[106]Sections 413ff.

[107]Sections 417f. Being seated on God's lap is an intensification in comparison to being seated "before the throne of glory" (section 411); see above, n. 105.

[108]Section 419.

characteristic of large sections of *Hekhalot Zuṭarti.*[109] Thereby, the impression is strengthened that (the) ascent traditions of *Hekhalot Rabbati* have been taken up in *Hekhalot Zuṭarti* and given a clearly theurgic flavor.[110]

109Cf. sections 335–374. The only passage in *Hekhalot Rabbati* where the heavenly journey and the adjuration are connected is sections 204f.

110The circle of the *yorede merkavah* is conceived most broadly in the difficult text section 420, where is mentioned the angel MGHShH who threatens the *yored merkavah* at the entrance to the first *hekhal,* and the angel PNYYWN, who opens the "gates of salvation" to grant "those who ascend to the Merkavah" (according only to MS New York; the other manuscripts read: "those who see him") grace and mercy: "Whoever sees him, whether bachelor or virgin, whether lad or old man, whether man [from] Israel or a gentile, whether servant or Israel, rushes towards him." The text displays the almost inseparable fusion of ascent and adjuration traditions in *Hekhalot Zuṭarti.*

4

Maᶜaseh Merkavah

God and His Name

The macroform called *Maᶜaseh Merkavah*[1] combines in its conception of God elements known to us from other texts, but at the same time, it also emphasizes certain features of its own, not least in the terminology.

It is self-evident that God sits on the throne of his glory, "in the chambers of the heights and in the palace of sublimity."[2] The

[1]The name *Maᶜaseh Merkavah* as the particular title of this macroform is not to be found in any of the manuscripts, but is based on Scholem's edition (*Jewish Gnosticism*, pp. 101ff.). Cf. both on this and the delimitation of the macroform, *Hekhalot-Studien*, pp. 13, 288ff., and *Übersetzung der Hekhalot-Literatur*, vol. 3, p. 237, n. 1.

[2]Section 544.

theology of the king, which plays such a major role in *Hekhalot Rabbati* in particular, is manifest here as well.[3] Concurrently, however, it is striking that the aspect of God's kingdom very often is connected to the emphasis placed on the power of the divine name; the latter, as we have seen, was one of the most outstanding characteristics of *Hekhalot Zuṭarti*. God is the omnipotent king, ruler over "those above" and "those below," and the power of this king, "whose name is like his power and whose power is like his name,"[4] is concentrated in his name or names:

> Your name is holy in the heavens of heavens,
> high and exalted over all of the Keruvim.
> Let your name be sanctified in your holiness,
> let it be magnified in greatness, let it be strengthened in might.
> And your reign [lasts] to the end of all generations,
> for your power is eternal, for time eternal.
> Praised are you, Lord, magnificent in strength,
> great in might.[5]
>
> May your name be praised forever and ever;
> your kingdom [lasts] from eternity to eternity.
> Your dwelling-place is eternal,
> your throne from generation to generation;
> your radiance is in heaven and earth.
>
> Your reign is over those above and those below.
> And everything presents in front of you song, praise, and hymn.
> Lord, your name is more righteous than everything.[6]

The glory of the king on his throne and the holiness and power of the divine name are also closely connected to one another that the texts in *Maʿaseh Merkavah* often read like an explication of the liturgical response to the uttering of the tetragram:[7] "Blessed be

[3]Cf. sections 548f.; 551ff., 555, 559, 562, 567f., 582, 587, 589, 591, 592f., 595.

[4]Section 557.

[5]Section 590.

[6]Section 591.

[7]Cf. m Yom 3:8 and more often; in the temple cult, the response to the uttering of the name of God by the high priest on the Day of Atonement, in the synagogue liturgy the response to the mention of the name of God in the first verse of the *Shemaʿ*

the name of the glory of his *kingdom* forever and ever."[8] The king, his name, and the necessarily resulting praise of the name form a recurrent triad:

> And above them all sits the king of the world,
> sitting on a high and exalted throne,
> and angels of glory comfort [him] with songs of praise,
> and those who shout in exultation
> and proclaim of his mighty deeds,
> stand at his right and at his left.[9] . . .
>
> Praised be [your] name,
> great, mighty and awesome,
> powerful, noble, daring and strong God,
> feared, wonderous and exalted God,
> who sits at the uppermost heights
> [and] who does his will in his world,
> and there is none, who will stop [him].[10]

A striking aspect in *Maʿaseh Merkavah* is the interest in the physical appearance of the heavenly world, which for the most part consists of fire. The bridges that lead over the rivers of fire are an important element of the heavenly geography;[11] God himself is consuming fire,[12] his chambers, his servants,[13] his throne[14] and his Merkavot in the seven *hekhalot*[15] are fire. From this it is self-evident that the name of God as well is connected to the element of fire. In

---

(see I. Elbogen, *Der jüdische Gottesdienst in seiner geschichtlichen Entwicklung,* 3d ed., Frankfurt am Main, 1931; reprint Hildesheim, 1967, p. 495).

[8]Cf. Sections 553, 555, 571.

[9]Cf. 1 Kings 22:19.

[10]Cf. Section 582.

[11]Sections 546, 559.

[12]This notion is biblical; cf. Deuteronomy 4:24.

[13]The fiery substance of the angels is also biblical (cf. Psalms 104:4; Judges 13:20; Daniel 10:6) and a common notion of rabbinic as well as Hekhalot literature; cf. BerR 78,1; ShemR 15,6; BamR 21,16; DevR 11,4; PesR ch. 16, fol. 80a (ed. Friedmann); ibid., ch. 33, fol. 155b; b Ḥag 14a and more often (see Schäfer, *Rivalität,* p. 51) and cf. in the Hekhalot literature, the transformation of Enoch into a heavenly being of fire (section 19) or phrases like "Keruvim of the fire" (sections 269; 692) and "Seraphim of the flame" (sections 2, 42, 72, 269, 553, 590, 776, 781, 801).

[14]Section 549.

[15]Section 554.

reference to Psalms 29:7 ("The voice of the Lord splits flames of fire") it is said of the divine name that it "splits with flames of fire" (*ḥoṣev*),[16] "wrapped (*meʿuṭṭaf*) in the fire of flames from fire and hail,"[17] even that it is "hewn [*ḥaṣuv*] in the fire of the flame."[18]

The concrete names of God as well, which are mentioned in *Maʿaseh Merkavah,* in part clearly are different from those in most other texts. Names such as RWZYY,[19] BRWKYY,[20] ʾNPRʾ,[21] ʾRKS,[22] or DDRYN[23] are found here almost exclusively and are characteristic of this macroform.[24] In an almost philosophical manner, the personal pronoun *hu* ("he [is]") is composed as the name of God:

> "He [is]" is his name,
> and his name is "he [is]";
> "he [is]" in "he [is],"
> and his name in his name . . . [25]

The favored name of God, in obvious reference to the terminology of the Shemaʿ, is "One" (*eḥad*):

> You are One,
> and your name is "One."[26]

> Great is your name in might, Lord,
> "One" is your name,
> and there is none but you.[27]

---

[16]Section 551. Cf. also *Sefer Yeṣirah* 2,2 (ed. Goldschmidt, p. 54), where it is said of the twenty-two letters: "He engraved them, split them (*ḥaṣavan*), purified them (or, placed them together)."

[17]Section 552.

[18]Section 549. The *ḥaṣuv* is difficult. If we are not to read *ḥoṣev* as in 551, then the meaning here likely is that it is made of fire, whereas in section 551 the concern is more with its effect.

[19]Sections 544, 547, 548, 595. The name can be derived from *raz,* "secret."

[20]Section 557. The name is to be derived from the root BRK, "to bless."

[21]Section 559.

[22]Section 564.

[23]Section 575.

[24]Only RWZYY is also to be found in *Merkavah Rabbah;* cf. sections 655, 656, 657, 821.

[25]Section 588.

[26]Section 589.

[27]Section 592, cf. also sections 562, 567, 593.

The highest stage of the unfolding of the divine name is the name which consists of forty-two letters, whose magical potency is used by the mystic:

> His name is expounded[28] in forty-two letters;
> he who performs it, is wise and wisdom fills [him].[29]

Angels

The Heavenly Praise

As in nearly all texts of the Hekhalot literature, the praise of God, in *Maʿaseh Merkavah* as well, is the privileged task of the angels; these are the same groups of angels with which we are familiar from the other macroforms:

> [In heaven][30] have you established your throne,
> you have placed your dwelling in the highest heights,
> your *merkav*[31] in the higher regions of your *zevul*,[32]
> in the light mist.
>
> The troops of fire glorify your remembrance,
> the Seraphim of fire sing your praise.
> In front of you stand the Ophannim and the *ḥayyot ha-qodesh*.
>
> And the Ophannim of majesty,
> the Seraphim of flame

---

[28]In the sense of "unfolds itself."

[29]Section 571. On the name of forty-two letters cf. b Qid 71a and sections 512, 516, 565, 625 (= adjuration of the *sar ha-panim*). See L. H. Schiffman, "A Forty-Two Letter Divine Name in the Aramaic Magic Bowls," *Bulletin of the Institute of Jewish Studies* 1 (1973): 97–102; Gruenwald, *Apocalyptic and Merkavah Mysticism*, p. 53, n. 81, and p. 174, n. 2; *Herkhalot-Studien*, p. 125 and n. 21.

[30]Only in MS New York 8128.

[31]*Merkav* is biblically in general the wagon, but also the palanquin of Solomon (Song of Songs 3:10).

[32]*Zevul* as a dwelling place of God is biblical (cf. 1 Kings 8:13; 2 Chronicles 6:2; Isaiah 63:15). In rabbinic and Hekhalot literature (there especially in the cosmological traditions), *zevul* is one of the seven heavens; cf. b Ḥag 12b and sections 21, 50, 439, 455, 721, 756, 772, and more often. See P. S. Alexander, "3 (Hebrew Apocalypse of) Enoch. A New Translation and Introduction," in J. H. Charlesworth (ed.), *The Old Testament Pseudepigrapha*, vol. 1: *Apocalyptic Literature and Testaments*, London, 1983, p. 239.

and the *galgalim* of the Merkavah
utter the name of God[33]
with a voice of great roaring,
trembling and quaking,
the name ṬṬRWSY YY',
one hundred and eleven times,[34]
and say . . . [35]

The name of God, which the angels know and pronounce, is the favored object of the heavenly praise:

This is your name for eternity
and such will you be named from generation to generation.[36]
Benevolent and merciful is your name,
your mercy is mighty
for those above and those below.
Your words are good
for those who love your Torah,
pure is your utterance
for those who sanctify your name. . . .

You have established your throne
with power, might, praise and song.
Clouds of fire,
hasty ones, who spread terror,
[and] adjutants, who instill fear,
a thousand thousands of thousands
and a myriad of myriads of myriads,
praise and glorify
your great, mighty and frightful name.
Before you stand all the mighty ones,
who are mighty in praise and in song.[37]

As in *Hekhalot Rabbati,*[38] the throne of glory also joins in the all-embracing song of the heavenly world:

---

[33]In Hebrew *omerim hazkarah. Lehazkir* and *hazkarah* in the Hekhalot literature denote the naming = uttering of the name of God (tetragram).

[34]On the number 111, see below, p. 112, n. 110.

[35]Section 590. There follow variations of ṬṬRWSY.

[36]Cf. Exodus 3:15 and Psalms 135:13.

[37]Section 549.

[38]See above, p. 13 and p. 61 (*Hekhalot Zuṭarti*).

Be magnified and sanctified
in eternity,
king, holy God,
high and exalted,
for there is none like you
in heaven and earth,[39]
in the sea and in the depths.
In the heights of *shaḥaq*[40]
your throne of glory sings. . . .
Ophannim of majesty
and Keruvim of holiness
sing a praise,
Clouds of comfort
[and] *ḥayyot ha-qodesh*
speak with song.
Their mouth is hail,
their wings water. . . .
Holy is your name,
your servants are holy.
Lord, One,
high and exalted God,
[with] joy and fear is filled
the throne of your glory.[41]

Gatekeepers

The classical function of the angels as guardians at the entrances to the seven *hekhalot* also is to be found in *Ma'aseh Merkavah,* however, it plays a much more subordinate role: the names of the guardian angels are not introduced in a concrete report or instruction of ascent, but are "expounded" by R. Yishma'el. Despite the narrative frame that refers to Yishma'el and Neḥunyah b. Haqanah, here we are dealing more with a descriptive enumeration[42] that culminates in the names of the angels who are

---

[39]Cf. 2 Chronicles 6:14.

[40]The *sheḥaqim* ("clouds") also belong to the seven heavens of rabbinic literature and the cosmological traditions of the Hekhalot literature; see above p. 81, n. 32.

[41]Section 593.

[42]Section 581.

situated directly to the right and left of the divine throne.[43] Only marginally do we otherwise learn that, on his ascent, R. ʿAqiva requested that the ministering angels should not destroy him.[44] To be separated from the ascent traditions are the "harmful spirits" (*maziqin*) who threaten man; they belong to the context of the adjuration traditions.[45]

Angels of Revelation

By far the most dominant task of the angels is the transmission of revelation. God granted the angels permission to "bind themselves" (*lehizzaqeq*) to man:

> You formed mighty ones of wisdom,
> who have permission
> to bring down the hidden of wisdom
> by the authority of your name.[46]

The names of these angels of revelation are known in part from other Hekhalot texts, in part, however, they are found only within *Maʿaseh Merkavah;* the result therefore is similar to that concerning the names of God. We learn of Suriya, the Prince of the Countenance[47] and Yofiʾel,[48] the Prince of Torah,[49] of various angels of the countenance,[50] of Meṭaṭron,[51] of Sandalphon, who "binds" the crown, respectively the Tefillin of God,[52] and of Mikhaʾel, the "Great Prince."[53] In addition, an otherwise unknown

---

[43]Section 582. One could even go a step further. Whereas in *Hekhalot Rabbati* the names of the angels are "merely" the means to the actual end of the heavenly journey, here the names themselves are the object of speculation. This naturally has consequences for the evaluation of the relationship of the macroforms to one another.

[44]Section 558.

[45]Sections 562, 568.

[46]Section 562. That is, the name grants permission, not God: God is his name.

[47]Sections 560; 581?

[48]From *yofi,* "beauty."

[49]Sections 560, 564.

[50]ShQDHWZYʾ = sections 561, 562, 584f.; ZRZRYʾL = section 582; ZBWDYʾL = section 583.

[51]Section 574; section 562 is ShQDHWZYʾ, "the servant" = Meṭaṭron?

[52]Sections 574, 582. Cf. also below p. 105.

[53]Section 576, section 578?

ZʿWPYʾL as the "Prince of the *gehinnom*" is mentioned[54] as well as an angel by the name of ʾRPDM.[55] An outstanding role is played by another angel known only to *Maʿaseh Merkavah,* the angel of the countenance PDQRM/PRQDS,[56] who is adjured by R. Yishmaʿel in a complicated ceremony; the revelation of wisdom (of the Torah) that the angel transmits is connected to certain prerequisites and takes place on earth:

> R. Yishmaʿel said:
> I asked for this secret and fasted twelve days.
> When I saw [however] that I could not [any longer] endure the fast,
> I made use of the great name [of] forty-two letters.
> Then PRQDS, the angel of the countenance, descended in anger,
> so that I trembled and fell backward.
>
> He said to me:
> Son of man, son of a stinking drop,
> son of vermin and worms,[57]
> you have made use of the great name— [this shall be] for you a lesson:
> I will give you the order of the Torah only
> when you have fasted for forty days.
>
> Immediately I stood up with all my strength
> and hurriedly issued from my prayer [the] letters,[58]
> and he ascended [again]:
> YH BYʾ RYBʾ BYʾ GDWLWT ʾTTBYH
>
> Then I fasted for forty days
> and each day I prayed three prayers at the [hour of] Shaḥarit prayer,
> three prayers at noon,
> three prayers at the [hour of] Minḥah prayer,

[54]Section 587. The name is derived from the root ZʿP, "to be angry with."

[55]Section 563 (with variations).

[56]With numerous variations; whether he is identical to ʾRPDM remains open. The meanings of both names are not clear.

[57]Cf. Job 25:6. On the complete phrase, cf. also section 313 (particular to MS Vatican 228).

[58]That are necessary to rid oneself of the angel and that are hereafter named.

three prayers in the evening
and mentioned [the] twelve words over each and every one of them.[59]

On the last day I prayed three prayers
and mentioned [the] twelve words.
Then PRQDS, the angel of the countenance, descended—
he and seventy angels [whom] he sent[60]—
and they caused wisdom to dwell in the heart of R. Yishmaᶜel.[61]

Man

Also in the relationship between man and God and man and the angels, *Maᶜaseh Merkavah* uses well-known elements from the other texts while at the same time emphasizing certain features of its own in a very typical manner. The outstanding characteristic, which weaves its way through the entire macroform, is prayer as the pivot of man's turning to the heavenly world, in regard both to the heavenly journey and the magic adjuration.

The Prayer as Means to the Ascent

In *Maᶜaseh Merkavah* as well, the most important protagonist of the ascent is R. ᶜAqiva.[62] Right at the beginning of the macroform, Yishmaᶜel asks ᶜAqiva for the prayer "one utters when he ascends to the Merkavah."[63] The prayer thereby obviously is the means that effects the ascent of the *yored merkavah*. Thus, it is stated tersely (likewise of ᶜAquiva):

---

[59]Apparently twelve magic words over each of the prayers.

[60]MS Oxford: "and with him angels of mercy."

[61]Section 565 (translation according to MS Munich 22).

[62]*Maᶜaseh Merkavah* often combines the otherwise mostly distinct Yishmaᶜel and ᶜAqiva traditions, whereby Yishmaᶜel obviously is subordinate to ᶜAqiva; see below, p. 88. This may as well be an indication of the more compilationlike character and later origin of the macroform.

[63]Section 544 in the version of MS New York. Once again the language (*ᶜoleh* instead of *yored*) is to be noted here; see above, p. 2, n. 4. Cf. also the beginning of section 81 (*Hekhalot Rabbati*), where R. Yishmaᶜel asks for the hymns "which one utters, . . . who wishes to ascend and descend unharmed." Do the Qedushah songs in *Hekhalot Rabbati* possess a similar function as the prayers in *Maᶜaseh Merkavah;* namely, as means to the ascent?

When I recited this prayer,
I saw 640,000 myriads of angels of glory
standing in front of the throne of glory,
and I saw the binding of the Tefillin of the hosts[64] of God,
and Lord, the God of Israel.
And I gave praise with all my limbs.[65]

The prayer not only causes the ascent—the procedure of the ascent plays no role whatsoever here and otherwise only a notably minor one, in crass distinction to *Hekhalot Rabbati*—it also is an essential element of that which the adept beholds (the binding of the tefillin by the angels) and at the same time the result of the vision: ʿAqiva praises God with all his limbs, and the praise is in this particular case none other than one of the central prayers of the synagogue liturgy, the ʿAlenu (however, with the remarkable change from the first person plural to the first person singular: "It is *my* duty to praise the Lord of all the things . . . ");[66] the most important themes of the praise, not surprisingly, are God's kingdom and the divine name.

The same structure is also found, for example, in section 592:

R. Yishmaʿel said:
Thus R. ʿAqiva said to me:
I recited a prayer and beheld the Shekhinah
and saw everything that one does before the throne [of glory].
And what is the prayer? . . .

The content of ʿAqiva's vision is described in somewhat more detail in the following passage, which apparently deals with the region above God on his throne (the eighth heaven?):[67]

R. Yishmaʿel said:
I said to R. ʿAqiva:

---

[64]The reference perhaps is to a *gedud* named Sandalphon (cf. section 655; below p. 104 and n. 46), who is responsible for God's tefillin; cf. sections 574, 582. The *gedudim* perhaps also are the "hosts" who accompany Sandalphon.

[65]Section 550; cf. also section 570.

[66]Section 551. See the extensive analysis by M. Swartz, "ʿALAY LE-SHABBEAḤ—A Liturgical Prayer in MAʿASEH MERKABAH," *JQR* 77 (1986/87): 179–190.

[67]Cf. section 100 (*Hekhalot Rabbati*); above, pp. 28f. and n. 67.

How can [one] see above the Seraphim
who stand above the head of RWZYY, the Lord,
the God of Israel?

He said [to] me:
When I ascended to the first palace, I recited a prayer
and saw from the palace of the first *raqia*ᶜ to the seventh palace.
And when I ascended to the seventh palace,
I mentioned [the names of] two angels
and beheld above the Seraphim. . . .

And when I mentioned [their names],[68]
they came and seized me.
They said [to] me:
Son of man, do not fear.
The holy king is he,
he who [sits][69] on a high and exalted throne.
Chosen is he in eternity and mighty over the Merkavah.

At the same hour I saw above the Seraphim
who stand above the head of RWZYY, the Lord,
the God of Israel.[70]

Here as well, there follows in detail the contents of the prayer ᶜAqiva recited on his ascent and that caused the described vision.[71]

The Protagonists of the Heavenly Journey

In a few passages, R. Neḥunyah b. Haqanah, R. Yishmaᶜel's "master," is mentioned as a protagonist of the heavenly journey in addition to R. ᶜAqiva.[72] R. Yishmaᶜel himself seems to form the bridge between the heroes of the past (ᶜAqiva and Neḥunyah b. Haqanah) and the "normal" *yored merkavah* and to transmit the experiences of the masters to the initiated adepts (about his own ascent remarkably we learn nothing whatsoever). In any case, *Maᶜaseh Merkavah* as well leaves no room for doubt that "man" (surely not

[68] Only in the manuscripts New York 8128 and Munich 22.
[69] Only in MS Munich 22.
[70] Section 595.
[71] Section 596: "And this is the prayer . . . "
[72] Cf. sections 556; 579; 586.

every man, but those who belong to the circle of the *yorede merkavah*) can imitate ʿAqiva and Neḥunyah b. Haqanah:

> Happy is the man
> who stands [firm] with all his strength
> and presents a praise before BRWKYY, the Lord,
> the God of Israel,
> and beholds the Merkavah and sees all
> that they do before the throne of glory,
> upon which BRWKYY, the Lord, the God of Israel, is seated.[73]

At the end of a long prayer section, it can then be summarized generally:

> "Anyone who recites this prayer with all his strength
> can behold the radiance of the Shekhinah,
> and the Shekhinah loves him.[74]

The Prayer as Means of the Adjuration

In *Maʿaseh Merkavah* prayer is not only a means toward the vision, but also (and above all) a means of the magic adjuration. As we have seen, the subject of this adjuration in the first instance is R. Yishmaʿel, who coerces the angel PDQRM/PRQDS to descend to earth through the mentioning of the forty-two lettered name, through fasting and prayer, so that he reveals to him the "order of the Torah"; that is, wisdom.[75] An important role in the adjuration of the angel apparently also is played by magic seals, which again consist of names and which the adjurer (in this case R. Yishmaʿel) lays on various parts of his body: on his heart, his feet, his two arms, his throat and his head.[76]

Without doubt, here R. Yishmaʿel likewise merely is the prototype and therefore the role model of those who perform the adjuration. It is stressed, more often than with regard to the heavenly

---

[73]Section 557.

[74]Section 591, MS New York. Literally, "And he will be beloved of the Shekhinah," which probably means, he loves the Shekhinah and the Shekhinah loves him.

[75]Section 565.

[76]Section 566.

journey, that "everyone" can adjure the angel and can "make use of the great mystery"; the contents are completely concerned with the secret of the Torah in the widest sense, that is, everything connected to learning, understanding, and remembering the Torah:

> The Prince of the Torah—Yofi'el[77] is his name.
> Everyone who longs for him, must sit for forty days and fast,
> eat his bread [only] with salt and not eat anything impure.
> He must perform twenty-four immersions and not look at any colors.
> His eyes must be cast to the ground,
> and he must pray with all his strength.
> He must submerge himself in his prayer
> and seal himself with his seals
> and mention [the] twelve words.[78]

The most important elements continually connected to the magic adjuration for the purpose of knowledge of the Torah are mentioned here: fasting, observance of particular purity rules concerning food, immersions, (sexual) abstinence, prayer, and seals. The special significance placed on concentration during prayer—eyes cast to the ground, *kawwanah*—is reminiscent of practices known to us from Sherira and Hai Gaon.[79]

The prayer recited by the adjurer can be recited in the style of the liturgical prayer and closely related to the classical language of prayer, or it can be combined with magical acts that far surpass the "pure" prayer. The following prayer text, in either this or a similar form, could be found as well in the *Siddur:*

> Whoever wants to make use of this great mystery
> must mention [the names of the] angels
> who stand behind the *ḥayyot ha-qodesh*...[80]
> And he must recite a prayer

---

[77]On the name Yofi'el cf. also sections 76 = 387, 277, 302, 313, 395, 397, 419, 628; and above, p. 84 and n. 48.

[78]Section 560. On the "twelve words" cf. also section 565; above, p. 86.

[79]Cf. B. M. Lewin, *Otzar ha-Geonim,* vol. 4, no. 2 (Ḥagiga), part 1 (Teshuvot), Jerusalem, 1931, p. 14; below, pp. 153f.

[80]There follow *nomina barbara.*

so that they do not destroy him,
for they are fiercer than all of the hosts of the heights.

And what is the prayer?
Blessed be you Lord, my God and creator,
great and awesome, living forever,
mighty over all the Merkavah.
Who is like you, mighty on high?
Let me succeed in all my limbs,[81]
so that I may reflect upon the gates of wisdom,
examine the ways of understanding,
behold the chambers of the Torah
and reflect upon [the hidden treasures of][82] the blessing . . .
Save me from all of them who stand fierce,
so that I will be beloved of them before you,
and I will know
that your holiness is forever.
Thus I will praise the holiness of your name forever
and sanctify your holy and great name.
May the great seal be on all of my limbs. . . . [83]

Here, only the last sentence reveals the magical connection; a much stronger magical tone is struck in the adjuration of the angel of the countenance 'RPDM:

Anyone who wishes to make use of this great mystery
must pray it with all his strength,
so that he forgets none of it;
all of his limbs would be [otherwise] destroyed.
And he must call those three names,
then I will descend. . . . [84]

There follows the enumeration of each of the mysterious names, respectively letters, that are reserved for the heavenly powers; they are an integral part of the prayer that adjures the "Prince of the Torah":

---

[81]The limbs sealed with the magic seals are meant.
[82]According to the manuscripts Munich 40, Munich 22 and Dropsie 436.
[83]Section 569.
[84]Section 563.

In the hour, when you pray,
pronounce [the] three names
that the angels of glory pronounce: . . .

And when you pray,
pronounce at the end [the] three letters
that the *ḥayyot* pronounce in the hour
when they behold and see ʾRKS, the Lord, the God of Israel: . . .

And when you recite another prayer,
pronounce [the] three letters
that the *galgalim*[85] of the Merkavah pronounce,
which sing a praise before the throne of glory: . . .

This is the acquisition of wisdom,
because everyone who pronounces these [names, letters]
acquires eternal wisdom.[86]

Finally, the emphasis can be placed so strongly in favor of the magical act that the original relation between prayer and the magical act resulting from it is in danger of being lost altogether. Particularly characteristic of this is a textual unit that only the New York manuscript transmits as a part of *Maʿaseh Merkavah*. Here, it is almost impossible to state to what extent we are dealing with "original" Hekhalot material or with "interpolations" of *ḥaside ashkenaz* traditions within the Hekhalot literature or "only" with magically underlined modifications of "original" Hekhalot texts by the *ḥaside ashkenaz*:[87]

Leaf of the fig tree:
I adjure you, Sandalphon,[88]
angel who binds the crown of his lord,

[85] The *galgalim* originally are the "wheels" of the Merkavah in Ezekiel 10:2.6, which here, however, are personified as a group of angels.

[86] Section 564.

[87] Cf. now K. Herrmann and C. Rohrbacher-Sticker, "Magische Traditionen der New Yorker Hekhalot-Handschrift JTS 8128 im Kontext ihrer Gesamtredaktion," *FJB* 17 (1989): 101–149.

[88] SWNDLPWN is likely an incorrect spelling of SNDLPWN (from the Greek *synadelphos*; i.e., someone who has a brother or who is a member of a fellowship); cf. also section 597.

to ascend and to say to him:
Two angels, Meṭaṭron and ʿGMTYʾ,
it is they, who [are] wisdom in the heart of that N.N.—
and [he] is knowing.

And I shall be wise and will understand,
complete and not forget,
learn and not forget . . .

Immerse in the evening and fast on the next day
and write on the leaf of a fig tree.
Eat [it] and drink thereafter wine
and sleep on your shoulder.

Leaf of the olive tree:
. . .[89]
These are the princes who split the *raqiaʿ*,
and they gave Moses the teaching through YHW YHW WHH.
I adjure you by his name . . . ,
so that you will preserve the teaching within my heart.
Write [it] on three leaves of the olive tree,
erase it with wine and drink.
Write the amulet and hang [it] on the left upper arm.

A cup of silver: . . .
These are the orders of Mikhaʾel,
the great [prince][90] of Israel,
which you should preserve for the study of the teaching in my heart,
Amen, Amen, Sela, Hallelujah.
Write [it] on a cup of silver,
erase [it] with wine and drink [the wine].
Then count fourteen times "listen to our voice,"[91]
and at the final one he should say:
"who hearkens the prayer."

Wine:
An open boil, which sits on your heart

---

[89] There follow *nomina barbara*.

[90] ʾYShRSW is likely a corruption of SRʾ.

[91] The sixteenth benediction of the ʿAmidah, which begins with "listen to our voice" and ends with "who hearkens the prayer."

and a deteriorating tumor, which sits on the opening of the
stomach . . . (?),
and throw upon me Bible, Mishnah, and Talmud
and enlighten my heart over the words of the Torah.
And I will not stumble in my speech,
in everything that I will learn, in the name of . . .
Say [this] forty one times over your own wine
at the beginning of the Sabbath,[92] when you lie,
and drink [from the wine];
on the next day, however, he should fast.

Egg:
. . .[93]
I am the great prince of the teaching,
who was with Moses on Mount Sinai. . . .
Everything that he learns
and everything that his ears heard—
so that you are able to do [it] and bring it to me
and that you may remove the stone from my heart,
as quickly as possible, and [do not hesitate],[94]
Amen, Amen, Sela.

Write on a one day old egg
from a black hen.
Roast this egg,
and after you have roasted it,
peel it.
And write on it,
on this egg,
this word,
and thereafter eat it
and do not drink thereafter.
On the same day he should fast,
and to be sure in (?) a box.[95]

The magical practice of writing names or formulas on certain objects, then erasing the formulas with a liquid and drinking the li-

[92] On Friday evening.
[93] There follow *nomina barbara*.
[94] Instead of *titᶜarev*, *titᶜakkev* should be read.
[95] Sections 574–578.

quid to "incorporate" the potency of the formula also is known from other sources[96] and appears to have been closely connected with the so-called magic bowls; what is unusual is that leaves from various trees are used as writing material (which were then obviously eaten) as well as eggs (which are eaten with the words written upon them, without drinking thereafter). The specifically Jewish form of this magical act is clearly illustrated by the fact that it always concerns the wisdom and knowledge of the Torah. Although the relation to the prayer remains merely a very loose one, there can be no doubt that the magical act is understood as a ritual-liturgical one. This is pointed to by the immersion and fasting, by the expressive mention of a benediction of the ʿAmidah (the hearkening of prayer), and by the temporal connection to the beginning of the Sabbath. Even the extreme form of the magic adjuration in *Maʿaseh Merkavah* is embedded in a, however individual, liturgical context (nowhere is a *community* made mention of here,[97] and it by no means has detached itself from the connection to "normative" Judaism.

---

[96]Cf. J. Naveh and S. Shaked, *Amulets and Magic Bowls. Aramaic Incantations of Late Antiquity*, Leiden, 1985, p. 16 and n. 11.

[97]Cf. I. Chernus, "Individual and Community in the Redaction of the Hekhalot Literature," *HUCA* 52, (1981): 262ff.

5

Merkavah Rabbah

God

God and His Name

The conception of God in the macroform *Merkavah Rabbah* is closely related to that in *Ma*ʿ*aseh Merkavah*. It goes without saying, that here as well, God as King is seated in the middle of his princely household on "a high and exalted throne," which is to be found "in the chambers of the heights, in the palace of sublimity";[1] this throne of glory is the "precious vessel" (*keli hemdah*) that God himself prepared.[2] However, this theology of the king, similar to that of

[1]Section 675; cf. also sections 655, 688, 691.

[2]Section 686. See also sections 94, 98f. (*Hekhalot Rabbati*); above, p. 13 and n. 7.

Maʿaseh Merkavah, is closely connected to the theology of the divine name; the center of attention is not so much the display of the might of the king in his princely household and as ruler over heaven and earth as the potency of his name or names.

Maʿaseh Merkavah equated "name" and "might" (*gevurah*)[3] and located the highest unfolding of the divine potency in the name *hu* ("he [is]").[4] In an analogous, and stylistically very similar, way, right at the beginning identifies *Merkavah Rabbah* the name with the divine countenance:

> His countenance [is] his name,
> and his name [is] his countenance,
> and the utterances of his lips [are] his name.[5]

The countenance of God, which in *Hekhalot Rabbati* played an important role as the goal of the *yored merkavah*'s vision,[6] here is reduced to the name or focused on it: one who "knows" the name also "perceives" the divine countenance; one need not really "behold" the countenance, it is sufficient to know the name, which contains all of the divine potency.

The name of God—together with certain magical acts—is prayed,[7] and also the angels who serve before the throne of glory "mention (*mazkirim*) your name":

> Blessed be the praise of your name
> and the song of your strength and your remembrance [*zikhrekha*][8]
> [in eternity] and forever.
> In the praise of your name
> is revealed the secret of wisdom
> and in the song of your remembrance [*zikhrekha*]
> are disclosed the mysteries of mysteries
> and the gates of understanding,
> so that the creatures of heaven and earth

---

[3]Above, p. 78.
[4]Above, p. 80.
[5]Section 655 according to the version in MS Munich 22.
[6]Above p. 16ff.
[7]Section 663; see below, p. 108.
[8]It is possible that with *zekher* (similar to *lehazkir* and *hazkarah;* see above, p. 82, n. 33) even the mention = uttering of the name of God is meant.

acknowledge before you:
Blessed be you, Lord,
wise of the mysteries
and ruler of all that is concealed.[9]

The result of the knowledge and praise of the divine name for the angels and (in particular) for man as well is the revelation of mysteries; the king, his name, and the praise of the name belong together as in *Maʿaseh Merkavah*. In comparison to *Maʿaseh Merkavah,* however, here it is emphasized more strongly that perception is connected to the name, the perception of hidden mysteries: one who "knows" the name of God and "mentions" it in praise (cf. the frequent use of the root *zakhar,* which always refers to the name) gains access to previously unknown and unobtainable sources of knowledge and understanding. This is why God often is praised as one who "reveals mysteries upon mysteries"[10] and whose praise culminates in the response "blessed be the *name* of glory of his *kingdom* forever."[11] God the king is "praised in the middle of names [*mehullal mitokh shemot*], for his names are sweeter than honey and milk."[12]

Shiʿur Qomah

In *Merkavah Rabbah* we encounter for the first time, as a separate and comprehensive literary unit within a macroform, the tradition of the *Shiʿur Qomah,* of the measurements and dimensions of the divine body.[13] R. Yishmaʿel desires to learn from the Prince of the Torah "the measurement of our creator,"[14] however, the measurements of God's limbs do not follow but a prayer of adjuration (which consists mostly of names)[15] as well as a Meṭaṭron passage (which lists the names with which the youth, i.e. Meṭaṭron, calls God).[16] Also in the second entry of the *Shiʿur Qomah* unit,[17] in

[9]Section 676.

[10]Section 675; cf. also sections 676, 687.

[11]Cf. sections 696, 702; above, pp. 78f (*Maʿaseh Merkavah*).

[12]Section 685 according to MS New York.

[13]On the redactional relationship between the *Shiʿur Qomah* traditions and the macroform *Merkavah Rabbah,* cf. *Hekhalot-Studien,* p. 28.

[14]Section 688.

[15]Section 689.

[16]Section 690.

[17]Section 691.

which it is proclaimed that the Prince of the Countenance, Meṭaṭron, will pass on "the measurement of our creator,"[18] the actual measurements at first are absent and instead the divine name is the main topic:

> Blessed be his great, mighty and frightful name,
> the clear and pure,
> the honored and noble,
> the strong, great and frightful,
> the clear, enduring and raised above the heights,[19]
> who resides upon the Keruvim of fire,
> who sits upon the Ophannim of flame,
> who rides forth on the *ʿaravot,*
> BYH is his name,[20]
> his pride is in the *sheḥaqim*
> and his name[21] is perpetual
> in eternity and forever.[22]

Next the name of God is mentioned (which consists mostly of variations of the tetragram) and once more praised with an eulogy:

> That is the name,
> the great, mighty and frightful,
> the powerful [and] pure,
> the honored and holy.
> Be praised, be sanctified,
> be extolled, be exalted forever,
> Lord, God of Israel,
> king of the kings of kings,
> praised be he.
> On a high and exalted throne do you reside,
> in the chambers of the heights
> of the palace of sublimity.
> For you revealed to Moses
> how one glorifies your name

[18]Section 692, MS Oxford.
[19]Instead of *meroman ʿal meromam* read *meromam ʿal meromim.*
[20]Psalms 68:5.
[21]According to MSS Oxford and Munich 40.
[22]Section 692 according to MS New York.

in fear, in purity and in holiness.
Amen, amen, sela.[23]

Only thereafter (quite suddenly) does the description of God's limbs follow, beginning with the soles of the feet and progressing over the shanks, thighs, shoulders, and neck to the head (hair, ears, forehead, eyes, eyebrows, nose, lips, tongue) and from there again over the shoulders to the arms, palms, fingers and toes; at the end, Song of Songs 5:10–16 is quoted, apparently analogous to this sequence and diverging from the biblical text.[24] Here, the names play an outstanding role as well. Not only is the size of each individual limb specified, but above all its name (often according to the "highest position," thus the characteristic point of the respective limb). Furthermore, the redactor obviously marked important caesuras in the text with the lists of names. Thus, for example, the redactor of MS New York inserted a list of seventy names between "shoulders" and "neck" that are "written" on God's heart, and ended this passage with the response to the uttering of the tetragram.[25] A further caesura is the description of the divine head, its measurements and its name, and of the crown on the head (whose name, in contrast to the otherwise *nomina barbara,* is given as *Israel*). We obviously are dealing here with a delimited redactional unit, as this passage ends with the remark "this is the stature of YDYDYH"[26] and likewise with the response "blessed be the name of glory of his kingdom forever."[27] A further insertion by the redactor of MS New York is to be found between "forehead" and "ears," this time a list of the seventy, respectively seventy-two letters (consisting for the most part of permutations of the tetragram) that are "written" on God's forehead.[28] Finally, in section 699 there appears to be a text fragment that in the present redactional context is incoherently inserted between "eyebrows" and "nose," but that originally may have marked a conclusion:[29]

---

[23]Section 694.

[24]Section 704.

[25]Section 696; cf. section 948.

[26]From *yadid* "beloved, friend"; cf. Isaiah 5:1; Jeremiah 11:15; Psalms 127:2.

[27]Section 697.

[28]Section 698. The redactor of MS New York obviously combined a number of sources or recensions with one another.

[29]Cf. the parallel in section 356.

The sight of his countenance
and the sight of his cheeks
is like the measure of the gentle breeze
and like the creation[30] of the breath of life.[31]
His radiance shines and is frightful
out of the darkness.
Cloud and fog surround him,
and all the Princes of the Countenance
are poured out before him
through the strength of the stature of his beauty and his embellishment.
We have in our hands no measurement (*middah*),
but the names are revealed to us.[32]

This final sentence might be the summary of a redactor who is "specifying" a significant aspect of the *Shi'ur Qomah* tradition in a formalized way: all attempts to "measure" and describe the *middot* of the creator are futile and illustrate the opposite of that which they want most to achieve; namely, that God's dimensions surpass any comprehensible "measurement" (a paradoxical effect that even is increased by the conversion of the divine parasangs to human measurements in section 703). The only thing man has are the names, which however, are, by no means insignificant, for not only are God's dimension revealed in these names, but his efficacy in the world as well. Despite the immense energy devoted to the scrupulous and sheer monstrous calculations of each individual divine limb in the *Shi'ur Qomah* tradition, in the end, the main concern is not the submersion of the mystic in the internal divine cosmos, but the power this cosmos exerts on the universe through the conveyance of his names. God is inconceivable in his stature, but he communicates with man by his names and thereby desires to be at his disposal.

The names of God found in *Merkavah Rabbah* offer no surprises. Variations of the tetragram and the *shem ha-meforash* dominate.[33] Particularly characteristic of *Merkavah Rabbah* is the

---

[30] *Kiṣirat* should be read in place of *biṣirat*.

[31] Here MS New York inserts: "No creature can recognize him. His body is like the Tarshish."

[32] Section 699, MS Oxford.

[33] On the latter, cf. sections 667, 670.

name RWZYY, or RZYY, with which the macroform begins[34] and whose obvious derivation from *raz* ("mystery") alludes to the leitmotif of the macroform.[35] The other concrete name (YDYDYH) likely belongs foremost to the context of the *Shiʿur Qomah* traditions; it is transmitted in this connection in *Merkavah Rabbah*[36] as well as in a *Shiʿur Qomah* passage that has been incorporated into a number of manuscripts of *Hekhalot Rabbati*.[37]

Angels

The Heavenly Praise

The role of the angels in *Merkavah Rabbah* is a notably insignificant one, perhaps the most insignificant of all the analyzed macroforms. It is presumed as self-evident that their main task is praising God; concrete angelic hymns are rare in *Merkavah Rabbah*. The otherwise so characteristic *Qedushah*, for example, is mentioned only once;[38] in comparison, benedictions are frequent, though they originate more with man than with the angels.

In accordance with the marked emphasis on the divine name, it is not surprising that precisely this name is the essential element of the angels' praise. In a long list we learn which angels praise God in which heaven:[39] the tradition of the seven *reqiʿim* is taken for granted, but the angels who rule these *reqiʿim* are not gatekeepers (and man as well makes no attempt to ascend through the seven heavens to the throne of glory); they are simply named as individuals who in heaven *X* praise God with the "words" *Y*, and this praise consists exclusively of names (for the most part tetragram variations). The names of the angels—Mikha'el, Gavri'el, Sodi'el/Suri'el, Aktari'el, Repha'el, Bodi'el/Bori'el,[40] Yom[i]'el[41]—are for the most

---

[34]Section 655; cf. also section 657. This name otherwise is found only in *Maʿaseh Merkavah*; see above, p. 80.

[35]See below p. 107ff.

[36]Sections 697, 704.

[37]The only exceptions are section 243, MS Leiden (where YDYDYH is clearly a corruption of *yeridah*), section 374 (where YDYD YH should be read instead of YDYDYH) and section 427 (where YDYDYH apparently is the name of an angel).

[38]Section 682, where it seems rather anachronistic.

[39]Sections 664–670.

[40]Other variations are BRDYYWL and BZRYL'L; cf. section 209 where he is one of the guardians at the entrance to the third *hekhal*.

[41]"Day of God" or "my day is God"; found only here.

part familiar ones; however, it remains unclear why a certain angel (with certain variations of the divine name) is located in a certain *raqia*ʿ.[42] In any case, *Merkavah Rabbah*'s message is a rather simple one:

> A thousand thousands over thousands
> and myriads over myriads
> stand and serve before the throne of glory
> and mention [*mazkirim*] your name.[43]

The angels praise God, but instead of the usual overflowing descriptions of their hymn, it is tersely stated that they "mention" the name of God (and there again follow variations of this name). The names with which Meṭaṭron "calls" God are individually listed,[44] however; they too consist primarily of permutations of the letters of the tetragram and as such do not differ from the names of the other angels. The fact that Meṭaṭron, in contrast to all the other angels, knows the very special name of God is little more than a pattern whose original contents appear for the most part to have been lost.[45]

Sandalphon and Meṭaṭron

Apart from the previously mentioned angels, who are mentioned rather incidentally, the dominant angels in *Merkavah Rabbah* are Sandalphon and Meṭaṭron. Sandalphon opens the macroform in a passage that is difficult to interpret: he is the *gedud*[46] who reaches "from the earth to the *raqia*ʿ"[47] and who also is known from the

---

[42]Cf. also section 21 (3 Enoch), where likewise seven angels are placed in charge of the seven *reqi*ʿ*im*. Among these angels are Mikha'el and Gavri'el as well; however, in 3 Enoch they are allocated to the seventh and sixth *raqia*ʿ, respectively, and in *Merkavah Rabbah* to the first and the second.

[43]Section 676.

[44]Section 690.

[45]This also supports the argument for a later stage of transmission and thus has consequences for the relative chronology of the macroform *Merkavah Rabbah*.

[46]The *gedudim* are known to later biblical literature (cf. Job 25:3; Sirach 48:9) as the hosts of the angels and also are found often within the Hekhalot literature (frequently as *gedudim shel za*ʿ*am*, respectively *za*ʿ*af*, "hosts of anger"; cf. sections 10, 384; 729; 957). The *gedud* in singular is the angel Sandalphon.

[47]Section 655; cf. also section 821.

Talmud.[48] There, the Ophan "on the ground next to each of the four-faced creatures"[49] is interpreted as an angel named Sandalphon "who stands on earth and whose head reaches to the *ḥayyot*". In the Talmud and the traditions connected to it,[50] his task is to stand "behind the Merkavah" and to bind "crowns for his creator." The parallels clearly show that these "crowns" consist of Israel's prayers, thus, for example, Midrash Konen:[51] "his name is Sandalphon and he binds crowns for the Lord of glory out of [the prayers] 'holy',[52] out of 'blessed be he'[53] and out of 'Amen, his great name be [blessed]'."[54] Quite different is *Merkavah Rabbah:* here the concern is not the prayers which are placed on God's head in the form of the crown, but the divine tefillin, which God himself (?) has put on[55]—however, not in order to pray, but to swear and to "throw" an oath on the earth, and as such, apparently to curse Israel. At this very moment, Sandalphon removes "the tefillin from his [i.e., God's] head and annuls [in this way] [the] restrictive laws from the earth."[56] This is a curious interpretation of the talmudic tradition: God puts on his tefillin to issue an oath, and Sandalphon nullifies this action against Israel by removing the tefillin from God (without which he apparently is "powerless"). Just as he sees to it in the Talmud that God is crowned through Israel's prayers (and thereby induced to be merciful), in *Merkavah Rabbah* he "strips" God of his magical potency

---

[48]b Ḥag 13b.

[49]Ezekiel 1:15.

[50]Cf. the analysis of the pertinent passages in K.-E. Grözinger, *Ich bin der Herr, dein Gott! Eine rabbinische Homilie zum ersten Gebot (PesR 20)*, Frankfurt am Main, 1976 [FJS 2], pp. 159ff.

[51]Jellinek, BHM II, p. 26. Cf. also PesR 20, fol. 97a (ed. Friedmann), where the threefold *Qedushah* (from the verses Isaiah 6:3; Ezekiel 3:12 and Exodus 15:18–Psalms 146:10) is related to the ritual of the crown. The Sandalphon motif is apparently connected to various liturgical traditions, from which *Merkavah Rabbah* decidedly differs.

[52]Of the *Qedushah* of Isaiah 6:3.

[53]Likely of the response *barukh hu u-varukh shemo.*

[54]Of the *Qaddish.*

[55]In section 574 (*Maʿaseh Merkavah*) Sandalphon binds the "crown (*taga*) of his master"; in section 582 (*Maʿaseh Merkavah*) he binds the tefillin "on the head of the rock of the world, of the Lord, of the God of Israel." The underlying notion probably is that God likewise puts on the tefillin when Israel prays. It is almost impossible to decide whether in *Merkavah Rabbah* God himself puts on the tefillin or whether Sandalphon puts them on him and then takes them off.

[56]Section 655.

(and prevents Israel's condemnation). As such, Sandalphon in both cases, albeit in a very different form, is Israel's intercessor.

Apart from this, we learn further in *Merkavah Rabbah*[57] only that R. Yishmaᶜel asks R. ᶜAqiva about Sandalphon's secret (*razo*). The answer consists of Sandalphon's name and numerous *nomina barbara* as well; that is, not only the name of God stands in the center of the macroform *Merkavah Rabbah,* but the names of the angels also are important.[58] That this also is true of Meṭaṭron is less surprising, as the relevance applied to his numerous names is well-known from other macroforms.[59] The familiar names of Meṭaṭron likewise are listed in *Merkavah Rabbah*[60] and equated with the divine name.[61] The names of God and of Meṭaṭron flow into one another, and apparently there is a tendency to include other angels in this identification process between the names of God and those of his angels (and in the magical potency derived from these names). Characteristic of this process is the following formula:[62] "the servants[63] are adjured with their king[64] and the servant[65] is adjured with his master."[66]

Angels of Revelation

The classical function of the angels as guardians at the entrances to the seven *hekhalot* no longer plays any role whatsoever in *Merkavah Rabbah;*[67] instead, the dominant task of the angels, as in *Maᶜaseh Merkavah,* is the conveyance of revelation. The Prince of the Torah,[68] respectively the Prince of the Countenance,[69] teaches Yishmaᶜel "the measurement of our creator" (= *Shiᶜur Qomah*);

---

[57]Apart from the macroform *Merkavah Rabbah,* Sandalphon is mentioned only in Section 597, MS Oxford (obviously a gloss that does not belong there).

[58]This is also displayed by the fact that later redactors entitled the macroform *Razo shel Sandalphon;* cf. section 597 and Musajoff, *Merkavah Shelemah,* fol. la.

[59]Cf. for example sections 4; 74; 76; 310; 396; 405; 487 and more often.

[60]Sections 682, 685.

[61]Section 685 (cf. section 277, *Hekhalot Rabbati*); in section 682, the *Qedushah* with Isaiah 6:3 follows the names of Metatron.

[62]Section 681.

[63]The angels.

[64]God.

[65]Meṭaṭron.

[66]God.

[67]See above, p. 103.

[68]Section 688.

[69]Sections 691 and 692, MS Oxford.

and based on the context, there is every reason to believe that in both cases Meṭaṭron is being referred to.[70] The adjuration of Meṭaṭron helps one toward "much study of the Torah"[71] and guards against forgetting the Torah:[72]

> I adjure you, Meṭaṭron,
> servant [of our creator],[73]
> whose name is like that of his master's,
> that you bind yourself unto me,
> in order to effect my desire,
> so that my countenance will shine,
> my stature will delight me,
> all beings will be filled with fear of me,
> my good name will circulate in all of Israel's places,
> my dreams will be pleasant to me,
> my Torah will be kept within me
> and no word from my mouth and from my heart will be forgotten
> from this day on [and in the future].[74]

Man

In *Merkavah Rabbah,* the connection between man and the heavenly world in emphasized in a characteristic way that separates this text from the other macroforms. The heavenly journey is forced completely into the background; the relationship between man and God, and man and the angels, instead is determined almost exclusively by the transmission of a "mystery"[75] that, although not explicitly described or named, can be ascertained from the context.

The Mystery of the Divine Name

We first learn of the mystery in the opening paragraph of *Merkavah Rabbah,* which introduces the decisive theme of the

---

[70]In section 686 Meṭaṭron is responsible for the study of the Torah (see below); the Prince of the Countenance in section 691, based on the names that follow, clearly is Meṭaṭron.

[71]Section 686.

[72]Section 706; cf. also section 705, below, pp. 115.

[73]Inserted in MS Oxford only.

[74]A gloss in MS Oxford; in the other manuscripts "and until the next day."

[75]The terminology is mixed: in addition to *raz, middah* is used, or merely *davar.*

macroform: God is his name. Directly thereafter we read: "A man who makes use of this mystery will . . . "[76] In this connection there can be almost no doubt that the mystery consists of the knowledge of the divine names. The Merkavah mystic "makes use" of these names and the "use" of the names produces certain results.[77]

Because the names of God and his angels are closely connected to one another, as has been shown, the mystery that man uses also can consist of the names of angels: "A man who uses this mystery and the names of the angels . . . "[78] In a similar manner the next paragraph: "A man who wishes to use this thing and the names of the angels . . . " Here, "thing" (*davar*) doubtlessly is identical with "mystery" (*raz*); perhaps, the phrases even are to be taken literally, consciously mentioning the names of the angels *in addition* to the "mystery" related to the name of God.

Not only does man "use" the mystery, that is, the names of God and the angels,[79] he "prays" it as well: "At the hour when you come to pray this name . . . "[80] The same liturgical context also can be seen in phrases such as "happy is he who brings this mystery from morning prayer to morning prayer to an end [*yigmor*]," that is, learns;[81] "every scholar who learns [*yilmad*] the great mystery";[82] "he who repeats, i.e. learns [*shoneh*] this great mystery, he should learn [this] Mishnah every day after his prayer. He should say it in purity at home or in the synagogue."[83]

Who Uses the Mystery?

The subject of the transmission and use of the mystery is both R. Yishmaᶜel[84] and "every man" (*adam*), respectively "every scholar" (*talmid hakham*);[85] R. ᶜAqiva is not present in this con-

---

[76]Section 655.

[77]See below, p. 114ff.

[78]Section 657.

[79]Cf. also sections 681, 683; section 682: "Every scholar who knows [*yodea*ᶜ] this great mystery."

[80]Section 663; section 670: When one mentions the name in purity, the prayer will be heard.

[81]Section 675.

[82]Section 687.

[83]Section 706; cf. also section 705.

[84]Sections 656, 677, 681, 688.

[85]Sections 655, 657, 681, 682, 683, 687, 705, 706.

nection (only in the triad Yishmaᶜel = student, Neḥunyah b. Haqanah = teacher, and ᶜAqiva = mediator).[86] The emphasis clearly is placed on the transmission of the mystery from R. Yishmaᶜel to "everyone":[87] each individual can use the mystery with success, just as R. Yishmaᶜel did; one merely must conform exactly to his role model. The transmission of the mystery occurs through the traditional teacher–student relationship, from Neḥunyah b. Haqanah via Yishmaᶜel to "every scholar." In this sense, the classical chain of tradition from *Pirqe Avot*[88] can be interpreted as pointing to the further transmission of the mystery to "all of Israel":[89]

> You revealed [them][90] to Moses,
> Moses to Joshua,
> Joshua to the elders,
> the elders to the prophets,
> the prophets to the pious,
> the pious to the God fearing,
> the God fearing to the men of the great assembly,
> and the men of the great assembly revealed [it] to all of Israel.

The Magical Use of the Name

The texts in *Merkavah Rabbah* leave no room for doubt that the "use" of the mystery is a magical action connected to certain conditions and combined with magical practices. Most important in this connection is writing down the names of God and the angels, for example in the following cryptic instruction:[91]

> Give me five shepherds,[92]
> and I will give them [a share] of this matter [*ba-davar ha-zeh*][93]

---

[86]Cf. section 681.

[87]Cf. in particular section 681.

[88]m Av 1, 1.

[89]Section 676.

[90]The plural follows from the pleonastic phrase "mysteries of mysteries of mysteries" at the end of the preceding paragraph. The introduction of this paragraph, however, clearly shows that "this mystery" is meant, which forms the theme of *Merkavah Rabbah*.

[91]Section 657; cf. also section 658.

[92]Cf. Ezekiel 34:1ff.; Zachariah 11:4ff.; Song of Songs 1:8.

[93]*Davar zeh* again is a synonym of *raz zeh*, the "[great] mystery."

and of the names of the angels,[94]
which he[95] writes down due to his authority [*ʿal reshuto*].[96]
He should mention [*yizkor*] two [names],
two [of them] he should [mention] seated,
two standing,
and he should mention the name RZYY,
the Lord,
the God of Israel,
before he writes them down.
If he writes them down without mentioning [*azkarah*],
his heart will succumb to folly.

A separate unit of tradition in *Merkavah Rabbah*[97] deals with magical actions carried out at particular times (ʿAṣeret,[98] New Year, each individual month [new moon], the month of Adar). The connection between the magical actions and the respective times remains vague (a relation to matters of the calendar seems to prevail); however, the meaning is obvious. In all cases, names (of God)—composed of variations of the tetragram and *nomina barbara*—are to be written on certain materials and then the names are to be physically "incorporated" in the truest sense of the word; the practice thereby corresponds to the one which we already have witnessed in *Maʿaseh Merkavah:*[99]

ʿAṣeret:[100]
Write these [names] on myrtle leaves
on the eve of ʿAṣeret.
When the cock crows one should put the myrtle leaves into his mouth
and erase them.

New Year:[101]
Write these [names] on bay leaves

[94]Thus, here as well the names of the angels are combined with the mystery of the names of God.

[95]The Merkavah mystic.

[96]Whose authority remains unclear: that of God or the angel?

[97]Sections 659–663.

[98]The last day of various festivals or in particular Shavuʿot.

[99]See above pp. 92ff.

[100]Section 660.

[101]Section 661.

on the eve of the New Year.
When the cock crows one should put the bay leaves into his mouth
and erase them.

Each month:[102]
Write these [names] on your fingernails,
put your fingernails into your mouth
and erase them.[103]

The first of Adar:[104]
Write these [names] in a bowl of silver,
pour wine into it
and [so] erase the letters with wine.

A magical formula[105] summarizes concisely the preparatory actions and magical practices and clearly reveals the liturgical connection:[106]

Purify yourself seven days,
wash [yourself] three times daily in the river
and purify yourself from bad food and from wine.
And in the hour
in which you come
to pray this name,
put a rolled up leaf [?][107]
into your mouth
to first chew it.
Thereafter pray:
Blessed be your name . . . [108]

Of further importance, in addition to writing down the names to be able to incorporate them, is the correct pronunciation of the

---

[102]Section 662.

[103]MS New York here adds: "You should do this three times. Eat salt in addition, three times a closed fist full. One should drink water and erase them [thus in the place of the corrupt "silence them"]".

[104]Section 663.

[105]Entitled *she'elah.*

[106]Section 663.

[107]The text is here corrupt; perhaps "Galil leaves."

[108]There follow permutations of the tetragram.

names; that is, the correct number and sequence. R. Yishmaᶜel is instructed by his teacher Neḥunyah b. Haqanah how to make use of "this mystery" (here, *middah*) and, without incurring injury, how "to adjure with it":[109]

His mouth brought forth names,
while the fingers of his hands counted
until he had counted one hundred and eleven[110] times.
And so everyone,
who makes use of this mystery [*middah zu*]:
His mouth should bring forth the names,
and the fingers of his hands should count
until he has counted one hundred and eleven times.
He should not leave out nor add any name.
Has he left out or added names,
his blood be on his own head.

The degree to which the magical practice of the "great mystery" is embedded in the traditional liturgy is illustrated by the following text:[111]

Every scholar
who knows this great mystery
should lie in his bed in the evening and recite the Shemaᶜ,
and [likewise] in the morning.
At the first vigil
and at the ninth hour of each day and in the night,
he should get out of his bed,
wash his hands and feet two times with water
and anoint them with oil,
put on tefillin
and pray standing before his bed.

---

[109]Section 681.

[110]The number 111 is a fixed sum for the repetition of the names; cf. sections 310 (*Pereq R. Neḥunyah b. Haqanah;* in MS Vatican 228 only); 590 (*Maᶜaseh Merkavah;* MS New York 8128 here raises the number to 112, apparently following the example of sections 214f.); MS Antonin 186, fol. 1a, 1.22 (= *Geniza-Fragmente zur Hekhalot-Literatur,* p. 165). *Hekhalot Zuṭarti* alone (sections 204f.) evidences the number 112 in all the manuscripts of the *Synopse*. It is uncertain how precisely the number 111, respectively 112, was arrived at and likewise unclear how this difference came about.

[111]Section 682.

When he has ended his prayer,
he should sit again on his bed
and say, interpret, adjure,
mention, decree, and fulfill
ShQDHWZYH . . . [112]

Although the liturgical ritual surely is not in accordance with the usual regulations (notable are for example the times for prayer—for the Shemaʿ?—in the daytime and at night), nonetheless it is obvious that the redactor places great importance on the connection of the "great mystery" (which again consists of uttering God's and Meṭaṭron's names) with reciting the Shemaʿ. Of a similar manner is another passage,[113] where an adjuration of Meṭaṭron is concluded with six benedictions, the first corresponding not incidentally to the fifteenth or sixteenth benediction of the ʿAmidah: "Blessed are you, Lord, who hearkens [the] prayer."[114]

In only a small number of passages in *Merkavah Rabbah* are ethical qualities named, which one who wishes to make use of the mystery must bring along; these are clearly influenced by Pinḥas b. Yair's "stages of holiness" in m Soṭa 9,15:[115]

In what manner does man use this thing [*davar zeh*]?
In fright,
in fear,
in purity,
through immersion,[116]
in sincerity,
in separation,
in humility
[and] in fear of sin.[117]

---

[112]There follow various names which are equated with the name of Meṭaṭron.

[113]Sections 706f.

[114]It is likewise no coincidence that the macroform *Merkavah Rabbah,* section 708, concludes with the request to hearken the prayer.

[115]See P. Schäfer, *Die Vorstellung vom Heiligen Geist in der rabbinischen Literatur,* Munich 1972 [STANT 28], pp. 118ff.

[116]That is, that he takes a ritual bath beforehand.

[117]Section 683; cf. also sections 659; 675; and 558 (*Maʿaseh Merkavah*). See N. A. van Uchelen, "Ethical Terminology in Heykhalot-Texts," in J. W. van Henten et al. (eds.), *Tradition and Re-interpretation in Jewish and Early Christian Literature. Essays in Honour of Jürgen C. H. Lebram,* Leiden, 1986, pp. 250–258.

Mastering the Torah

What is the result of the revelation of the "great mystery," which consists for the most part in the names of God and the angels and its use by man? *Merkavah Rabbah* here mentions various effects, all of them, however, pointing to the same goal: complete and unbroken knowledge of the Torah.

The man who "uses this mystery" is praised as being happy, for "he knows the orders of heaven and earth and he extends [his] days to eternal life."[118] Similarly section 675: "Happy is the man who brings to an end this mystery from morning prayer to morning prayer. He acquires this world, the world to come and worlds upon worlds." The Merkavah mystic, to whom the mystery is revealed, is certain not only of being a child of the world to come (i.e., that he will be redeemed), but moreover, the present world is transformed for him and his life takes on a completely new meaning:[119]

When my ears heard this great mystery,
the world was transformed over me in purity
and my heart was,
as if I had arrived in a new world;
Every day it appeared to my soul,
as if I was standing in front of the throne of glory.

This experience of the new "identity" of the Merkavah mystic also can be described by the metaphor of light:[120]

When he revealed to me [the] names [of the] angels,
I raised myself
and engraved them due to [the] authority [?],[121]
and there was a light in my heart[122]
like the light of a flash
which goes[123] from one end of the world to the other.

---

[118]Section 655.

[119]Section 680.

[120]Section 656; cf. also section 657.

[121]The phrase is a difficult one, however, it appears to be concerned in particular with "writing down" the received names; see above pp. 109f.

[122]Cf. section 580 (*Maʿaseh Merkavah*).

[123]Thus *holekh* instead of the corrupt *ḥolekh*.

The dimension of the new experience of the Merkavah mystic that is transmitted through the "mystery"—his "enlightenment," the transformation of the present, and the firm belief in salvation in the future world—can mean only one thing for the conception of the world in the Hekhalot literature: the constantly desired and never realized absolute certainty in everything related to the Torah.[124] The mystery that God revealed to "all Israel" causes Israel to (truly!) fulfill the Torah and increase the teaching.[125] A poetic passage summarizes concisely what awaits one who knows the "great mystery" and how to use it correctly:[126]

> He who learns [*shoneh*] this great mystery,
> his countenance will shine,
> his stature will delight him,
> the fright of him will lie upon all creatures,
> and his good name will circulate in all of Israel's places;
> his dreams will be pleasant to him,
> and his Torah will be kept within him:
> all the days of his life he will not forget the words of the Torah.
> Happy be he in this world
> and pleasant in the world to come!
> Even the sins of his youth will be pardoned in the future.
> The evil inclination will not control him
> and he will be saved from the spirits, demons, and robbers,
> from all evil animals,
> snakes and scorpions,
> and from all evil spirits.

The Adjuration

Apart from the revelation of the "mystery," so characteristic of this macroform, *Merkavah Rabbah* also is acquainted with the classical adjuration whose goal is protection against forgetting the Torah. A small and redactionally delimited unit (which in a number of

---

[124]Therefore, it is somewhat curtailed to equate the "mystery" with the "mystery of the Torah"; cf. *Hekhalot-Studien,* p. 30. In reality, the mystery consists of the names of God and the angels, and the knowledge of the Torah is the *result* of the use of this mystery.

[125]Section 676; cf. also section 657.

[126]Section 705; cf. also section 706, above p. 107.

manuscripts also is transmitted in *Hekhalot Rabbati*),[127] informs us of the adjuration of Yishmaʿel through Neḥunyah b. Haqanah in the chamber of hewn stone (*lishkat ha-gazit*).[128] The result, as in the unit of the previously analyzed "mystery" traditions,[129] is revelation of the mysteries of the Torah and protection against forgetting them:[130]

> At once, R. Neḥunyah b. Haqanah, my master, stood up[131] in front of me,
> took me away from my father's house,
> led me into the chamber of hewn stone
> and adjured me with the great seal,
> which has ZBWDY'L, the Lord, the God of Israel,
> and this[132] is Meṭaṭron,
> the Lord, the God of Israel, . . .
> and revealed to me the secret and mystery of the Torah.
> At once he enlightened my heart in the eastern gates,[133]
> and my eyeballs beheld

---

[127] Sections 278–280; 308f. = sections 677–679, *Merkavah Rabbah*. It cannot be decided conclusively in which macroform this unit is "original," though there is much that favors *Merkavah Rabbah*.

[128] Based on tradition, the hall built of hewn stones in the Second Temple in which the great Sanhedrin convened. We obviously are dealing with a place of revelation, which is connected with the Holy Spirit or the Shekhinah (cf. sections 297; 202). Here, in *Merkavah Rabbah*, respectively *Hekhalot Rabbati*, the traditional concept of the revelation of the Holy Spirit or the Shekhinah in the temple is transferred to the adjuration ritual of the Merkavah mystic.

[129] Here, in contrast, the [great] mystery" is not named, although the seal doubtlessly consists of names. Hence, from the standpoint of redactional criticism, the traditions of the "[great] mystery" and the sections 677–679 (?) are to be differentiated. Section 680 once again takes up the theme of the "great mystery," and section 679 ("this mystery") perhaps forms the bridge between the two literary units (in MS Budapest, section 280 = section 679 belongs clearly to the Yishmaʿel-Neḥunyah b. Haqanah tradition, as it is defined by *tosefet*, "addition"). Even more complicated is the state of affairs in section 309, MS Vatican: there the otherwise separate tradition of section 680 is obviously built into the unit section 279 = section 678.

[130] Section 678; cf. also section 689, which also deals with the adjuration with the great seal and the great oath.

[131] Instead of the corrupt *ʿamadeti*.

[132] The seal is obviously meant, although the *zehu* also may refer to God. In any case, the text shows once more (also by placing "the Lord, the God of Israel" behind the name of Meṭaṭron), that it is almost impossible to differentiate between God and his angel.

[133] Of the temple; cf. also sections 202 and 297 (*Hekhalot Rabbati*).

the depths and the paths of the Torah.
Thereupon I forgot nothing of all
that I perceived with my ears from the mouth of my master
[and] from the mouth of the students . . .

The literary units of the "great mystery" and regular adjuration of an angel, which from the redactional point of view doubtlessly are to be separated, are combined at the end of the macroform:[134]

One who learns this great mystery,
should learn [this] Mishnah each day after his prayer.
He should say it in purity at home or in the synagogue:
I adjure you, Meṭaṭron,
servant [of our creator],[135]
whose name is like that of his master's,
that you bind yourself to me,
to effect my desire . . . [136]

The Ascent of ʿAqiva

The macroform *Merkavah Rabbah* is so pervaded by R. Yishmaʿel as protagonist, that the few cases where R. ʿAqiva appears independently (i.e., not only as "mediator" between R. Yishmaʿel and his teacher R. Neḥunyah b. Haqanah) can be viewed as redactional critical elements and give rise to doubt concerning the authenticity of the ʿAqiva passages.[137] In any case, it is noticeable that the only two textual units in *Merkavah Rabbah* in which ascent traditions in the sense of the classical heavenly journey are incorporated are connected with the name of ʿAqiva.

The first of these two passages is made up of two versions of the *pardes* story,[138] which also are transmitted in the macroform *Hekhalot Zuṭarti*.[139] Speculation about the "original" location of the

[134]Section 706; cf. also section 681, where it is explained how one "*uses* this mystery and how one *adjures* with it."

[135]Only in MS Oxford 1531 in parentheses.

[136]See above p. 107.

[137]Cf. *Hekhalot-Studien*, pp. 24ff.

[138]Sections 671–672, only in the manuscripts New York and Oxford; in MS Munich 40 shortened with "and so on" following the introductory sentence.

[139]Sections 338–339; 344–345; see above p. 68.

pardes story within the macroforms of the Hekhalot literature is of little use, as this passage, being a clearly defined (though by no means always identical) redactional unit, obviously was so important to the redactors of the Hekhalot manuscripts that it could be integrated into various contexts. In *Merkavah Rabbah,* however, it appears to be of a secondary nature. The same is true of the immediately following sections 673 and 674, which are redactionally much more securely anchored in *Hekhalot Zuṭarti* than *Merkavah Rabbah.* The writers of both the manuscripts that evidence section 674 in *Merkavah Rabbah*[140] were acquainted with the tradition from another context, as they shorten the text with "and so on" following the introductory sentence.

Of great interest is the second passage, which, after an introduction,[141] describes an actual heavenly journey by ʿAqiva:[142]

> R. ʿAqiva said:
> When I went and asked this question before the throne of glory,
> I saw him, the Lord,
> the God of Israel,
> how he rejoiced with great joy,[143]
> stretched out his hand, his right,
> and [with it] struck the throne of glory.
> And he said:
> ʿAqiva my son,
> this throne of glory
> on which I sit
> is a precious vessel,[144]
> which my hand, my right, established.

---

[140]MSS New York 8128 and Oxford 1531.

[141]Section 685: "R. ʿAqiva descended in order to expound the Merkavah [*lidrosh ba-merkavah*]." The phrase *lidrosh ba-merkavah,* which is clearly influenced by m Ḥag 2:1 (*en dorshin...ba-merkavah beyaḥid*), is very rare in the Hekhalot literature. Apart from this passage, it is found only in the Genizah fragment T.-S. K 21.95.A, fol. 1b, lines 10ff. (*Geniza-Fragmente zur Hekhalot-Literatur,* p. 175): "R. Eliʿezer [*ha-gadol*] expounds the Merkavah [*doresh ba-merkavah*]; R. ʿAqiva explores [*mefallesh*] the Merkavah, [R. Ḥananyah b.] Ḥakinai tells [*mesapper*] about the Merkavah."

[142]Section 686.

[143]Cf. on this motif of God's joy over the *yored merkavah* sections 216 and 218 (*Hekhalot Rabbati*), above pp. 40f.

[144]On the throne as *keli hemdah,* cf. sections 94; 154; above p. 13 and n. 7.

Even to a non-Jew [*ger*]
who has just now converted to Judaism,
whose body is pure
of idolatry, bloodshed, and illicit sex,[145]
will I bind myself [*ani nizqaq lo*].
Meṭaṭron, my servant, I will bind him [*ani mazqiq lo*]
to his footsteps
and to much study of the Torah.
When I departed from the throne of glory
to descend [*laredet*][146] to man,
he said to me:
ʿAqiva, my son,
descend [*red*]
and bear witness of this mystery [*middah*] to the creatures.
Then R. ʿAqiva descended [*yarad*]
and taught the creatures this mystery [*middah*].

Here, at first, it is striking that the actual heavenly journey is reduced to the pale (and unusual) phrase "when I went." The ascent proper plays no role whatsoever. This is illustrated as well by the fact that the term *yarad,* which otherwise is so typical for the ascent, is here used ingenuously for the return from the throne of glory.

Curious furthermore is the connection of God's right hand with the throne of glory. In section 164 (*Hekhalot Rabbati*) God's hands (not the right one) lie upon the arms of the figure of Jacob that is engraved on the throne (?); in 3 Enoch, God holds his right hand concealed behind his back due to the destruction of the temple.[147] Whereas in 3 Enoch we are dealing with a gesture of calamity, here the concern is unequivocally a statement of salvation: God *takes an oath* with his right hand,[148] and indeed clearly *on the throne of glory,* the "precious vessel," established precisely by this right hand.

---

[145]Cf. section 199 (*Hekhalot Rabbati*). Idolatry, illicit sex, and bloodshed are the three Noachide laws often named in representation of all seven; cf. M. Kadushin, "Introduction to Rabbinic Ethics," in *Jehezkel Kaufmann Jubilee Volume. Studies in Bible and Jewish Religion . . . on the Occasion of His Seventieth Birthday,* Jerusalem, 1960–61, p. 96; and (on their use in the Hekhalot literature) van Uchelen, "Ethical Terminology in Heykhalot-Texts," pp. 253ff.

[146]On the terminology cf. above p. 2, n. 4.

[147]Section 68.

[148]The right hand is the hand of oath; cf. also section 638.

The content of the oath is remarkable in two ways. For one, it connects the traditional elements of the adjuration with the unit of tradition of the "mystery," so characteristic of *Merkavah Rabbah*. Meṭaṭron, with whom God "binds"[149] man—and this implies nothing other than the connection of God himself with man[150]—helps toward "much study of the Torah," thus toward the complete mastering of the Torah. The text, therefore, is a combination of "mystery" and adjuration traditions[151] that on their part are integrated into an ascent tradition in a very peculiar way. This doubtlessly is the attempt of a (later) redactor to bring the two units of tradition into harmony with one another.

Furthermore, another notable aspect of the text, which is unusual not only for *Merkavah Rabbah* but for the entire Hekhalot literature, is the promise of the obtainment of knowledge of the Torah through the adjuration of Meṭaṭron not only to the *yored merkavah* as member of a particular group nor only to all Jews, but expressly even to the non-Jew who has converted to Judaism and adheres to the seven Noachide laws.[152] This already is hinted at in *Hekhalot Rabbati*,[153] although we are certainly not dealing there with a *yored merkavah* who has converted to Judaism; the expression *ger* in the Hekhalot literature is evidenced solely in this passage of *Merkavah Rabbah*.[154] Whereas the phrase "non-Jew" who has converted to Judaism" (*ger she-nitgayyer*) clearly refers to the convert, the proselyte, the additional description "whose body is pure of idolatry, bloodshed, and illicit sex" brings to mind a broader notion of *ger*. The seven Noachide laws are the minimal ethical demands made on all people, that is, also and especially non-Jews,[155] and therefore are not exactly appropriate in defining the demands made on the proselyte

---

[149]On the magical terminology of ZQQ, cf. I. Gruenwald, "Qetaʿim ḥadashim mi-sifrut ha-hekhalot," *Tarbiz* 38 (1968–69): 365, n. on l. 31, and *Hekhalot-Studien*, p. 259.

[150]Meṭaṭron and God are "identical"; see also above p. 116 and n. 132.

[151]Cf. section 706; above p. 117.

[152]The three laws mentioned very likely stand as *pars pro toto* for all seven Noachide laws; see above p. 119, n. 145.

[153]Section 199. On *Hekhalot Zuṭarti*, section 420, see above, p. 75, n. 110.

[154]An interesting parallel in rabbinic literature is SER ch. 10, p. 48 (ed. Friedmann): "Be it a non-Jew [*goy*], be it a Jew; be it a man, be it a woman; be it a servant, be it a maid—upon each lies the Holy Spirit according to the deed which he performs." Cf. Schäfer, *Die Vorstellung vom Heiligen Geist*, pp. 131f.

[155]Cf. *EJ*, vol. 12, cols. 1189ff., s.v. Noachide Laws.

who has converted to Judaism.[156] Therefore, *ger* perhaps is not to be understood as referring to the proselyte but rather to the *ger toshav;* that is, one who has expressly taken upon himself the obligations of the Noachide laws.[157] In any case, this text (along with *Hekhalot Zuṭarti,* section 420) is the one that most openly formulates the Hekhalot literature's propagated ideal (heavenly journey and adjuration): the exclusive privilege of an elite group becomes accessible to "all of Israel,"[158] where *Israel* is understood in the widest sense possible, including the *gerim*.

---

[156]Apart from four of the Noachide laws, section 199 mentions "evil slander," "perjury," "impudence," groundless hostility," and particularly "all mandatory commandments and prohibitions"; i.e., clearly shows that the concern is the entire Torah.

[157]Cf. b AZ 64b; see *EJ,* vol. 15, col. 421, s.v. Strangers and Gentiles.

[158]Cf. also the reinterpretation of the Avot chain in section 676; above, p. 109.

6

3 Enoch

God

The Shekhinah on the Throne

In comparison to the other Hekhalot texts the conception of God in 3 Enoch is strikingly traditional. This is displayed first of all by the terminology employed: 3 Enoch has a clear preference for expressions such as *the Holy One, blessed be he,* the *dwelling place* (*maqom*), and above all *Shekhinah,* God's "residence" in certain places among man; thus, terms well-known from the classical rabbinic literature.[1] All of these terms indeed are present as well in the other Hekhalot texts, though by no means are they so dominant as in

[1]Cf. A. Marmorstein, *The Old Rabbinic Doctrine of God,* Oxford 1927–37; S. Esh, *Der Heilige (Er sei gepriesen). Zur Geschichte einer nachbiblisch-hebräischen*

3 Enoch. On the other hand, the term *king*, which is particularly characteristic of the Hekhalot literature, is seldom found in 3 Enoch.[2]

God's Shekhinah rests in the seventh *hekhal*, thus in the highest, or if we imagine the arrangement concentrically innermost of the seven heavenly "palaces," which themselves are to be found in the highest (= seventh) heaven. Specifically, God sits, or his Shekhinah rests, on the "throne of glory" (*kisse ha-kavod*),[3] which itself stands on the Merkavah (the "chariot" of Ezekiel 1), or the "wheels of the Merkavah."[4] It is said of Yishmaᶜel, for example, that he enters the seventh *hekhal*, is led to the "camp of the Shekhinah," and presented before the "throne of glory" to behold the Merkavah;[5] similarly, Meṭaṭron serves the "throne of glory, the wheels of the Merkavah, and the needs of the Shekhinah."[6]

Whereas the Merkavah remains strangely vague—it is more presumed than described—the "throne of glory" also plays a central role in 3 Enoch; one sometimes gathers the impression that the throne, though not more important, is more tangible than God himself. Thus, R. Yishmaᶜel wishes to "say [a song] before the throne of glory of the king of glory" and not before the "king of glory";[7] shortly thereafter he says "a hymn before the throne of glory," and the "holy creatures below the throne of the king of glory and above the throne"[8] answer him.[9] Meṭaṭron does not serve simply God, but the throne of glory;[10] and one of his special distinc-

Gottesbezeichnung, Leiden, 1957; A. Goldberg, *Untersuchungen über die Vorstellung von der Schekhinah in der frühen rabbinischen Literatur*, Berlin, 1969 [SJ 5].

[2]Cf. Sections 1; 2; 4; 39.

[3]In addition the traditional biblical notion of God who "sits on the Keruvim" (cf. section 34; see Psalms 80:2, 99:1; 1 Samuel 4:4; 2 Samuel 6:2; 2 Kings 19:15; Isaiah 37:16; 1 Chronicles 13:6) or who "rides" on the Keruvim (cf. the conclusion of section 37 and the beginning of section 38. The only verse that speaks of God riding on the Keruv is Psalms 18:11 = 2 Samuel 22:11; 3 Enoch falsely quotes [or interprets] Isaiah 19:1: *rokhev ᶜal-ᶜav qal*. The quotation possibly also is a combination of Isaiah 19:1 and Psalms 18:11 or 2 Samuel 22:11).

[4]Cf. section 19; see Ezekiel 10:2.6.

[5]Section 2.

[6]Section 19; cf. also section 10: "where the throne of the glory of the Shekhinah [is found] and the chariot".

[7]Section 2.

[8]The notion of the holy creatures *above* the throne of glory is a strange one not evidenced elsewhere.

[9]Ibid.

[10]Sections 10f.; 19: the throne of glory, the wheels of the Merkavah and the needs of the Shekhinah—in this order!

tions is the fact that God makes a throne for him "like the throne of glory."[11] A particular angelic prince writes Israel's merits "on the throne of glory,"[12] other angels "know the mysteries of the throne of glory."[13] The Seraphim, one of the highest classes of angels, radiate "like the splendor of the throne of glory, which even the holy creatures, the majestic Ophannim, and the glorious Keruvim cannot look upon, for the eyes of anyone who looks on it grow dim from its great brilliance."[14]

As already has been stated, the Shekhinah rests on the throne of glory; however, this too is more presumed than described. Of particular interest to the redactor of 3 Enoch are the questions *why* the Shekhinah rests in the highest heaven in the seventh palace and *how* it got there. To these questions is devoted one of the introductory sections,[15] which very clearly picks up on and incorporates older rabbinic traditions:[16] after the expulsion of Adam from paradise, the Shekhinah at first rested on a Keruv beneath the tree of life, while Adam sat at the entrance to the garden of Eden and (still) nourished himself on the splendor of the Shekhinah:

> The first man, however, and his generation sat at the entrance to the garden of Eden so that they might gaze at the bright image of the Shekhinah, for the brilliance of the Shekhinah radiated from one end of the world to the other, 65,000 times [brighter] than the wheel of the sun; for anyone who makes use of the brightness of that Shekhinah is not troubled by flies or gnats, by sickness or pain, and all kinds of evil spirits cannot harm him.[17]

It was first the generation of the Enosh, the grandchildren of Adam, who brought idolatry into the world,[18] that caused the Shekhinah to depart forever from the earth and man and that justified

---

[11]Section 13.

[12]Section 26.

[13]Section 27.

[14]Section 42.

[15]Sections 7f.

[16]See Goldberg, *Schekhinah*, pp. 13ff.

[17]Section 7. See Goldberg, ibid., p. 289.

[18]On this unit of traditions cf. P. Schäfer, "Der Götzendienst des Enosch," in *Studien zur Geschichte und Theologie des rabbinischen Judentums*, pp. 134ff.

the angels who from the start were against man and against God's presence with them:

> Why did you leave the heavens of the highest heavens, the abode of your glorious name, the high and exalted throne which is in the height of *ʿaravot,* and come and dwell with the sons of Adam, who worship idols and put you on par with idols?! Now you are on the earth, and the idols are on the earth—what is your business among the inhabitants of the earth, the idol worshipers?! Immediately the Holy One, blessed be he, took up his Shekhinah from the earth, from their midst.[19]

Transcendence of God?

In 3 Enoch, the presupposed situation thus is that of God, who is far away from the world and man and who reigns in the highest heavens: God had been among men, but withdrew his Shekhinah due to their sins. As such, it is legitimate to speak of God's transcendence in 3 Enoch. I tend to doubt, however, whether this is the principle conviction of 3 Enoch and the entire Hekhalot literature, an opinion that once again has been expressed by P. Alexander.[20] In particular, I do not believe that one can base this on the statement that God has withdrawn his Shekhinah from the earth and that he is "represented as being well-nigh inaccessible to man."[21] The God who reigns in the highest heaven so difficult to reach is only half of the story; more exactly, it is the presupposition of the message in 3 Enoch. The metamorphosis of the man Enoch into the highest angel Meṭaṭron, which is described in the first major section of the book,[22] is meant precisely to show that God remains accessible, that man not only can reach God, but that he can become almost his equal. True, Enoch does not remain a man, he must be transformed into an angel;[23] however, the text leaves no

[19]Section 8.

[20]"The basic assertion about God in 3 Enoch and in the other Merkabah texts is that he is transcendent," Alexander, "3 (Hebrew Apocalypse of) Enoch. A New Translation and Introduction," in *The Old Testament Pseudepigrapha,* vol. 1, p. 241.

[21]Alexander, ibid.

[22]Sections 4–20.

[23]Cf. *Hekhalot-Studien,* pp. 274f.; a different explanation is provided by Gruenwald, *Apocalyptic and Merkavah Mysticism,* p. 201.

room for doubt concerning the human origin of the angel Meṭaṭron. Furthermore, the relation between God and man is twofold, to the extent that not only does Enoch become Meṭaṭron, but, in the presumed narrative frame, the man Yishmaʿel also ascends to God's Merkavah. As such, the statement of the book *as a whole* is the following: God *indeed* withdrew his Shekhinah from the earth and now reigns on his throne in the seventh palace in the seventh heaven and he will not return to earth; *however,* man—though not every man: Enoch-Meṭaṭron as the prototype of the past, R. Yishmaʿel as the prototype of the present—can ascend to him and see him seated on his high and exalted throne.

The Appearance of God

To be sure, we learn next to nothing concerning God's actual appearance on his throne; on this point, 3 Enoch is perhaps the least explicit text within the spectrum of the entire Hekhalot literature. The radiance of the Shekhinah is wonderful to behold and it shields Adam, as we have heard, from illness and misfortune. Beyond this, we learn only that the "radiance of the Shekhinah" lies on the countenances of the angelic prince Keruviʾel and the Keruvim subordinate to him;[24] this doubtlessly means that Keruviʾel and his Keruvim stand so close to the Shekhinah that its radiance is reflected on their faces.[25] Thus 3 Enoch hardly goes further than the classical rabbinic literature, which states that the angels nourish themselves on the radiance of the Shekhinah.[26] Neither are statements issued concerning the effect of the radiance on men nor even about other forms of the appearance of God on the throne.[27]

The Names of God

Finally, the treatment of the names of God (and the angels) in 3 Enoch also matches this finding. Whereas other Hekhalot texts are almost overflowing with a texture of partly intelligible, partly unintelligible names (*nomina barbara*) that are difficult to disentangle

---

[24]Section 34.

[25]One cannot place this in direct relation to section 42, where the Keruvim are unable to even look at the radiance of the throne of glory.

[26]Cf. for example PesK 6, 1, p. 110 (ed. Mandelbaum) = PesR 16, fol. 80a (ed. Friedmann); PesR Appendix, fol. 194a; see Goldberg, *Schekhinah*, pp. 281ff., 526ff.

[27]At best indirectly, by way of the enthronement of Meṭaṭron in analogy to God.

and surpass one another in their theurgic potency, 3 Enoch, with its well-ordered and "serious" disposition, is very reserved in this respect. The names of God are mentioned in detail in only one passage, whose affiliation to 3 Enoch is considered doubtful:[28]

> These are the names of the Holy One, blessed be he,
> which go forth [crowned] with many crowns of flame,
> with many crowns of
> *ḥashmal*,
> with many crowns of lightning flash,
> with many crowns of lightning[s],
> from before the throne of glory;
> with them [go] a thousand camps of the Shekhinah
> and myriads of hosts of the strength [*gevurah*];
> they escort them[29] like a king . . . ,
> give to them honor and strength[30]
> and cry before them: Holy, holy, holy [Isaiah 6:3] . . .
> They roll them through every single *raqiaʿ* in the height
> like mighty and noble sons of kings,
> and when they bring them back to the place of the throne of glory,
> all the *ḥayyot* beside the Merkavah open their mouths
> in praise of the glory[31] of the name of the Holy One, blessed be he, and say:[32]
> Blessed be the name of glory of his kingdom for ever and ever.[33]

This theology of the divine name has no theurgical or magical potency whatsoever. The names are part of a heavenly liturgy—here again the connection to the throne of glory is to be noted—which in the truest sense of the word revolves within itself and, being self-sufficient, does not establish a connection to man.

---

[28]On the affiliation of sections 71–80 to 3 Enoch, cf. Alexander, "3 (Hebrew Apocalypse of) Enoch," p. 310, n. a.; idem, "Appendix: 3 Enoch," in Schürer, Vermes, and Millar, *The History of the Jewish People,* vol. 3.1, p. 272; Schäfer, *Hekhalot-Studien,* pp. 230f.

[29]According to MS Munich 22.

[30]According to MS Munich 22: *ʿoz* instead of *ʿonim.*

[31]According to MS Munich 22.

[32]According to MS Munich 22.

[33]Section 71.

Angels

One is able to state without exaggeration that the angels (or more precisely, the heavenly world) are (or is) the central theme of 3 Enoch. In no other text of the Hekhalot literature do we find such a richly ordered and so obviously systematized angelology. Although different systems, which in part can be harmonized only with difficulty, likewise are combined here, the endeavor of the redactor toward uniformity, toward the design of a comprehensive heavenly hierarchy, is unmistakable.

The Angelic Hierarchy

The description of the angelic hierarchy begins in section 21 with the seven angelic princes who are placed in charge of the seven heavens (*reqiʿim*); there follows a list of the princes of the sun, the moon, the planets, the stars and the seventy-two, respectively seventy, gentile nations, which likely represent an individual tradition that the redactor has incorporated here. In the explicitly fixed order of these angelic princes (section 23, in an established formula[34] that evidently is characteristic of this whole angelological unit)[35] the seventy-two or seventy princes of the gentile nations stand above the prince of the seventh heaven. There follow the (anonymous) guardians at the entrances to the seven palaces (*hekhalot*) in the seventh heaven (*ʿaravot*) as well as the (likewise anonymous) four princes placed in charge of the four camps of the Shekhinah.[36] A long list of angels then follows, who are respectively placed one above the other and of whom the majority, as a sign of their rank, possess the letters of the tetragram as a component of their names. The list culminates with the two angels Soferiʾel YWY, who brings death, and Soferiʾel YWY, who revives (the names differing only in the letters *samekh* and *sin* as well as in the epithets *memit* and *meḥayyeh*) and who thus are placed in charge of the books of life and death, respectively.

[34]"The prince of the *raqiaʿ X*—when he sees the prince of the *raqiaʿ Y*, he removes the crown of glory from his head and falls upon his face."

[35]The combination of the princes of the seventy-two gentile nations with the princes of the *reqiʿim* obviously is secondary, for the princes of the sun, moon, planets, and stars are absent here.

[36]Section 24.

The next unit,[37] which is interrupted by various other pieces, presents the hierarchy of the angels who reside in the direct environs of the divine throne: Rekhavi'el, who is placed in charge of the wheels of the Merkavah; Ḥayyli'el, in charge of the four holy creatures with their respective four faces; Keruvi'el, in charge of the Keruvim; Ophanni'el, in charge of the Ophannim; Seraphi'el, in charge of the Seraphim; an angel of uncertain etymology, in charge of the heavenly book archives; and finally, as the climax, the well-known "guardians and holy ones" (*ʿirin* and *qedishin*) from Daniel 4:10.14:

> Their region is opposite the throne of glory, their location opposite the Holy One, blessed be he, so that their region radiates like the throne of glory and the brilliance of their appearance is comparable to the brilliance of the Shekhinah. . . . And not only this, the Holy One, blessed be he, does nothing in his world without first taking counsel with them; only thereafter does he act, as is written: This sentence is decreed by the watchers [*ʿirin*]; this verdict is commanded by the holy ones [*qedishin*] [Daniel 4:14].[38]

The Heavenly Praise

With the exception of the angels placed in charge of the book archives, as well as the guardians and holy ones connected to the divine court of law, the main task of all the other angelic princes mentioned here is to impel their subordinate angels to praise God. Thus it is said of Ḥayyli'el, the angel placed in charge of the four holy creatures,[39] that he "strikes the creatures with flaming blows, adorns them when they recite praise, hymn, and knowledge, and following the 'Holy, holy, holy' [Isaiah 6:3] impels them to say [the response] 'Blessed be the glory of the Lord in his place' [Ezekiel 3:12]."[40] Sim-

---

[37] Sections 30–34; 39–44, respectively 46. According to Alexander, "3 (Hebrew Apocalypse of) Enoch," p. 242 (see however idem, "Appendix: 3 Enoch," p. 271), the unit goes to ch. 28, 6 = section 44, however one can include sections 45 and 46.

[38] Section 44.

[39] The name of the angel thus stands for his function, the supervision of the *ḥayyot*.

[40] Section 31.

ilarly, in a particularly poetic example, Rekhavi'el,[41] who is responsible for the praise of the wheels of the Merkavah:

When the time comes to sing the hymn,
the multitude of the wheels trembles,
the multitude of the clouds shudders,
all the captains tremble,
all the horsemen are agitated,
all the heroes shiver,
all the hosts shake,
all the legions are afraid,
all the overseers[42] flee terrified,
all the princes and soldiers are panic struck,
all the servants are despondent,
all the angels and cohorts are whirled around:[43]
Wheel to wheel,
Keruv to Keruv,
ḥayyah to *ḥayyah,*
Ophan to Ophan,
Seraph to Seraph
let their voices resound:

Extol him who rides in the *ʿaravot,*
BYH is his name,
exult in his presence (Psalms 68:5).[44]

The recital of the daily hymn, which culminates in the trishagion from Isaiah 6:3, is the angels' foremost task. A further large thematic unit revolves around the description of what occurs in heaven during the angels' recital of the powerful, heaven- and earth-shaking "Holy, holy, holy."[45] When the angels recite the trishagion in the correct manner (*ketiqno*) they are crowned with splendid

---

[41]Here as well, the name of the angel alludes to his function, the supervision of the praise with Psalms 68:5 (*sollu la-rokhev ba-ʿaravot*).

[42]According to MS Vatican 228 instead of *hamonim* ("masses") in MS Munich 40.

[43]*Mitḥolelim* seems here to be understood as in Jeremiah 23:19: "a whirling storm, it shall whirl down upon"; Odeberg, ad loc.: "travail with pain"; Alexander, "3 (Hebrew Apocalypse of) Enoch," ad loc.: "writhe in agony".

[44]Section 30.

[45]Sections 53–58.

crowns; however, when they make the slightest mistake (meaning that they fail to recite the trishagion in perfect harmony), God extends his little finger and burns them: "Then the Holy One, blessed be he, opens his mouth, speaks one word and creates others instead of them, [others] like them, new ones. Each of them then stands in song before the throne of glory and recites 'Holy,' as is written: 'They are renewed every morning,[46] ample is your grace' [Lamentations 3:23]."[47]

The description of the angels and their heavenly praise for the most part is an end in itself, man is not present therein. However, based on the narrative frame and the constantly repeated opening formula: "R. Yishmaᶜel said: the angel Meṭaṭron, the Prince of the Countenance, said to me," the entire macroform is shown to be a revelation of Meṭaṭron to R. Yishmaᶜel, who for his part has ascended to heaven. At the beginning it is stated explicitly that R. Yishmaᶜel himself sings a hymn before the throne of glory, the holy creatures joining in with the trishagion of Isaiah 6:3 and the "Blessed be the glory of the Lord in his place" (Ezekiel 3:12).[48] Therefore, there can be no doubt that in 3 Enoch as well the praise of the angels in heaven serves as the model for earthly praise, even though the connection is less direct than in other texts and determined mostly by the narrative frame. It also is notable that the otherwise so frequent Merkavah hymns are fully absent in 3 Enoch, a fact that has been correctly evaluated as indicating the antitheurgic tendency of 3 Enoch.[49]

Meṭaṭron

Of the numerous angelic princes, whose functions not always are clearly separated from each other and who have assumed differ-

---

[46]Every morning the angels are renewed.

[47]Section 58; see also section 67 and above, pp. 26f. (*Hekhalot Rabbati*). Rabbinic literature is acquainted with the tradition that, with his little finger (!), God burns the angels who oppose his wish to create man; cf. b San 38b and parallels and Schäfer, *Rivalität,* pp. 95ff.

[48]Section 2. The song, however, is not his own, but rather given to him by God. Cf. section 251 (*Hekhalot Rabbati*), where the successful adept who has made his way to the seventh *hekhal* joins in the daily praise of the throne of glory.

[49]Alexander, "3 (Hebrew Apocalypse of) Enoch," p. 245. I would not want to see this as a result of the "final redaction of this work," however, but rather to the contrary, it appears to me that the antitheurgic tendency belongs to the core of the book and its essential assertion.

ent filiations, Enoch = Meṭaṭron is the most important. He is the central figure in the first part of the book,[50] to a certain degree the link between the earthly and heavenly worlds. His task is to serve the throne of glory,[51] and to fulfill this task, he is transformed into the greatest of all angels.[52] His throne ("like the throne of glory") is placed at the entrance to the seventh palace.[53] He receives a special garment (in *Hekhalot Rabbati,* God's garment as goal of the Merkavah mystic's vision plays an important role)[54] and a crown in which God engraves the letters with which heaven and earth were created with his finger, as though with a flaming style.[55] As the "lesser YHWH," he is God's representative[56] ("Each and every angel and each and every prince who has anything to say before me[57] shall step forth before him[58] and speak to him. Each and every word he says to you in my name, you must observe and do"), like God omniscient: "All the thoughts [in] the hearts of men, all the mysteries of the world and all the orders of the creation were revealed to me[59] just as they are revealed before the maker of creation. . . . Before a man thinks in secret, I see [it], before a man acts, I see [it]. Nothing in the height or in the deep of the earth is concealed from me."[60]

It is interesting to briefly compare this statement about Meṭaṭron with a text from the so-called *gedullah* passages in *Hekhalot Rabbati.* What is here said of Meṭaṭron, there belongs to the special privileges of the *yored merkavah,* thus to the *human* who ascends to the divine throne in the seventh palace:

> The all surpassing greatness [of the *yored merkavah*] consists of
> his recognition and knowledge of every human act,
> even [those] that they perform in the chambers of chambers,

---

[50]Sections 1–20.

[51]Sections 10f., 19.

[52]Section 12.

[53]The opposition to this special status of Meṭaṭron is expressed in the incorporation of the Aḥer tradition (section 20), according to which Meṭaṭron is punished by *ʿAnafiʾel* (see above, p. 31 and n. 83); cf. also the polemic in b Ḥag 15a.

[54]See above, p. 19.

[55]Sections 15f.

[56]Section 13.

[57]God.

[58]Meṭaṭron.

[59]Meṭaṭron.

[60]Section 14.

be it virtuous or disgraceful acts.
If someone has stolen,
then he knows [it] and recognizes him,[61]
if someone performs adultery,
then he knows [it] and recognizes him;
if [someone] has slain a man,
then he knows [it] and recognizes him. . . . [62]

Meṭaṭron knows the thoughts and acts of men before they are performed, whereas the *yored merkavah* knows all the secret but accomplished sins of men, and yet this is only a gradual difference. Both the *yored merkavah* and Meṭaṭron possess a secret knowledge that otherwise is reserved for God alone, they are both almost like God. If one adopts the findings of recent studies[63] which suggest that 3 Enoch is to be placed rather at the end of the literary production of the Hekhalot literature, then a noteworthy development can be seen here: that which, in an earlier phase of Merkavah mysticism, was valid for the albeit limited and elite, yet nonetheless earthly, group of the *yorede merkavah* is confined in 3 Enoch to the one privileged man, Enoch, who has been transformed into the angel Meṭaṭron; it is, so to speak, remythified. Based on the background of the entire Hekhalot literature, the observation therefore is correct that the message of Merkavah mysticism again is rerouted into more traditional paths and "objectified," it acquires a greater distance. The self-consciousness of the *yored merkavah,* which perhaps is most comprehensible to us in the *gedullah* passages of *Hekhalot Rabbati,* is broken and has been transferred to the single and special man who has been transformed into an angel. Actually, R. Yishmaᶜel only imitates this angel Enoch-Meṭaṭron; that which Meṭaṭron has to say (and show) to him is decisive, not what he himself experiences and learns.[64]

---

[61]The thief.

[62]Section 83; see above, p. 41.

[63]Cf. Alexander, "3 (Hebrew Apocalypse of) Enoch," pp. 226ff.; idem, "The Historical Setting of the Book of Enoch," *JJS* 28 (1977): 156ff.; idem, "Appendix: 3 Enoch," p. 274; Schäfer, *Hekhalot-Studien,* pp. 221ff.

[64]Even Meṭaṭron is relativized, as his special status is criticized; cf. sections 13 and 20 as well as above, n. 53.

Man

The Heavenly Journey of the *yored merkavah*

From what has been said up to this point, man's status in 3 Enoch follows conclusively. The ascent of the *yored merkavah,* who overcomes numerous dangers in reaching the throne of glory in the manner of the Hekhalot literature, is minimized to the narrative frame of the opening paragraphs; besides the portrayal of Enoch's elevation and the hierarchy of the angels, the major part of the book is taken up by the description of the heavenly geography,[65] which follows the example of the heavenly journey of the classical apocalypse under the guide of an "angelic interpreter" (*angelus interpres*). The individual segments of tradition always are introduced by the formula "Meṭaṭron said to me: come, I want to show you . . . I went to him, he took me by the hand, lifted me upon his wings and showed me." In this manner R. Yishmaʿel sees the letters with which heaven and earth were created,[66] various prodigies,[67] the souls of the righteous,[68] wicked and the intermediate,[69] the curtain before God's throne in which are woven all of the past and future acts of man,[70] the stars and their names,[71] the souls of the burnt angels who did not sing the Qedushah correctly,[72] and the right hand of God, which he holds concealed behind his back due to the destruction of the temple and which he will bring out in the future to redeem Israel.[73]

---

[65]Sections 59–70.

[66]Section 59.

[67]Section 60.

[68]Section 61.

[69]Section 62.

[70]Sections 64f. Cf. also sections 346 (*Hekhalot Zuṭarti*) = 673 (*Merkavah Rabbah*) and in particular T.-S. K 21.95.J, fol. 2b, lines 2f. (= *Geniza-Fragmente zur Hekhalot-Literatur,* p. 133). On the rabbinic and other parallels, cf. O. Hofius, *Der Vorhang vor dem Thron Gottes,* Tübingen, 1972 [WUNT 14]; Gruenwald, *From Apocalypticism to Gnosticism,* pp. 210ff.; Alexander, "3 (Hebrew Apocalypse of) Enoch," p. 296, n. a.

[71]Section 66.

[72]Section 67.

[73]Sections 68–70. On this motif with parallels in rabbinic literature (EkhaR Pet. 24, fol. 13a [ed. Buber]) cf. now M. Fishbane, " 'The Holy One Sits and Roars': Mythopoesis and the Midrashic Imagination."

Eschatology and Anthropology

This is the conclusion of the main part of 3 Enoch (a number of sections follow that clearly differ in style and content and whose affiliation to 3 Enoch is disputed),[74] which completely follows the traditional redemption theology of the early Jewish and rabbinic apocalypses. In the end, God will redeem Israel from the gentile nations, the Messiah will appear and bring Israel to Jerusalem. There, Israel will gather from all four corners of the earth and together with the Messiah (and the gentile nations!) will partake of the messianic feast.[75]

Thus, like the classical early Jewish and rabbinic literature, 3 Enoch is concerned primarily with the fate of Israel and those connected to it, although the emphasis is placed more on the individual than Israel as a nation; neither a resurrection of the dead at the end of time nor a general last judgment is mentioned. Each individual will be judged by his deeds,[76] his achievements will be written on the throne of glory[77] and placed on a scale before God;[78] the righteous will be given eternal life, the wicked death.[79] The souls of the righteous will return to God after the death of the individual,[80] the souls of the intermediate will be purified of their sins in the fire of She'ol (and then will likely be united with the souls of the righteous though the text remains silent concerning this), and the souls of the wicked will be judged in the fire of Gehinnom.[81] Here as well, it is not stated explicitly what will happen to them, though it is quite certain that their punishment is final and that they will remain forever in Gehinnom.

Thus, the anthropology of 3 Enoch essentially is based on traditional early Jewish and rabbinic anthropology. Man is responsible for his own fate and either rewarded or punished according to his good or evil deeds.[82] This certainly is not a theme particularly char-

---

[74]See above, p. 128, n. 28.

[75]Section 70.

[76]Probably directly following his death; cf. sections 43ff.

[77]Section 26.

[78]Section 27.

[79]Ibid.

[80]Section 61.

[81]Section 62.

[82]Cf. E. Sjöberg, *Gott und die Sünder im palästinischen Judentum nach dem Zeugnis der Tannaiten und der apokryphisch-pseudepigraphischen Literatur,* Stuttgart, 1938

acteristic of the Hekhalot literature; as such, the special role of 3 Enoch in comparison to the other "writings" of the Hekhalot literature here is confirmed as well.

It must be added however that this is true only for the textual form of 3 Enoch that we have before us at present; that is, following its redaction by Ashkenazi Jewry in the Middle Ages.[83] In a Genizah fragment I discovered and published, we find precisely the passage about the souls of the righteous, the intermediate, and the wicked to which I have referred. At first, it follows the hitherto known text word for word, but then deviates from it in a decisive manner. Directly following the judgment of the souls of the wicked in Gehinnom the fragment continues:

> And he showed me twelve constellations and also their zodiacs.... He said: One who is born in the constellation of Libra, on the first day [of the week], [under the dominion] of Jupiter or the moon, if the child is born in those two hours, it will be born small and tender and radiant. It will have a sign on the fingers of its hands and [on] the toes of its feet; or an additional finger will be on its hands or [an additional toe] will be on its feet. This person will be fast and will have three lines in [the form of] crowns on its forehead;... and the lines are wide, and he is one of the good. At the age of seven months and ten days he will be ill and will lie in warm water.[84]

Here we find ourselves quite unexpectedly in an astrological text with elements of metoposcopy and chiromancy (the interpretation of the lines of the forehead and the hands); similar traditions are otherwise known to us only from Qumran and medieval Jewish literature.[85] The decisive difference to the "classical" 3 Enoch is that

---

[BWANT 4, 27]; E. E. Urbach, *The Sages. Their Concepts and Beliefs,* 2d ed., Jerusalem, 1979, pp. 436ff.

[83]On the Ashkenazi redaction of 3 Enoch, cf. *Hekhalot-Studien,* pp. 228f.

[84]T.-S. K 21.95.L, fol. 2b, lines 13–21 = *Geniza-Fragmente zur Hekhalot-Literatur,* p. 137.

[85]Cf. G. Scholem, "Hakkarat panim we-sidre sirṭuṭin," in *Sefer Assaf. Festschrift Simḥa Assaf,* Jerusalem, 1952–53, pp. 459–495; idem, "Ein Fragment zur Physiognomik und Chiromantik," in *Liber Amicorum. Studies in Honour of Professor Dr. C. J. Bleeker,* Leiden, 1969, pp. 175–193; I. Gruenwald, "Qeṭaʿim ḥadashim mi-sifrut hakkarat-panim we-sidre-sirṭuṭin," *Tarbiz* 40 (1970–71): 301–319; P. Schäfer, "Ein

here the usual relation between guilt and punishment, merit and reward is not emphasized; rather man's fate is dependent on the constellation of the stars at the time of his birth, thus predetermined and furthermore, can be read by the learned from the lines on his hands or feet and on his forehead. The fragment thus shows that the art of astrology and the interpretation of the lines of the forehead and hands was cultivated in the very circles of the Merkavah mystics. Should this assumption be substantiated (the textual material is as yet too minute), then we would have a further and very impressive proof for the tendency, which is particularly evident in 3 Enoch, toward a renewed reflection on the traditional values of Jewish theology and the mitigation or even removal of those elements especially characteristic of the Hekhalot literature.

---

neues Fragment zur Metoposkopie und Chiromantik," in *Hekhalot-Studien,* pp. 84–95.

7

Results

Man between God and the Angels

The Hekhalot literature revolves around the relationship between God, the angels that surround him, and man. This formulation of the question certainly is not new; however, it is intensified and answered in a new manner. Not only do the individual macroforms display thoroughly different focal points, but the macroforms themselves by no means are monolithic blocks; they consist of redactionally formed layers with various currents and tendencies.

God

In the center of the theological cosmos of the Hekhalot literature stands God as reigning king on the throne of glory; this aspect is to be found in all the examined macroforms, albeit with very different degrees of emphasis. It is absolutely central in *Hekhalot Rabbati* with its numerous royal hymns. There, the concrete question in point is also the appearance of God on his throne; its beauty, which is concentrated especially on his countenance and in his garment, is the goal of the *yored merkavah*. The divine countenance is the center of a dramatic heavenly occurrence, in which participates the *yored merkavah,* who has ascended to the throne of glory. A distinct tension between the vision itself and the danger that stems from this vision is thereby unmistakable: the *yored merkavah* longingly desires this vision above all (and is expressly called upon by God to "descend" to him), and yet, no man—and no angel either—can endure the sight of the divine countenance and garment.

Hekhalot Zuṭarti likewise is familiar with the theology of the king and the ascent tradition connected to it, however, only in the redactionally well-defined layer of sections 407–426. In *Maʿaseh Merkavah* and *Merkavah Rabbah* it is mentioned, though rather marginally, and combined with the other central theme of the Hekhalot literature, the divine name. A special role (and not only here) is played by 3 Enoch: the divine throne is of great importance; however, on the throne is not seated the king, but the Shekhinah, the dominant manifestation of divinity from the classical rabbinic literature. The actual appearance of God also recedes into the background behind the description of the heavenly topography and hierarchy.

The might and potency of the divine names (and in part also the names of the angels) is emphasized in *Hekhalot Zuṭarti* (in the redactional layer sections 335–374) and clearly is the focal point of *Maʿaseh Merkavah* and *Merkavah Rabbah*. The names of God hold cosmic potency and effect wonders (*Hekhalot Zuṭarti*), the essence of God consists of names (*Maʿaseh Merkavah:* his name is his might and his might is his name).[1] Insofar as the divine countenance is equated with his name (*Merkavah Rabbah*), the heavenly journey becomes superfluous.[2] Knowledge of the divine name causes revelation and perception (of the Torah); for the most part this is

---

[1]On the theology of the name in *Maʿaseh Merkavah,* cf. now also Janowitz, *The Poetics of Ascent,* pp. 25ff., 83ff.

[2]The garment of God, which is covered with the tetragram in *Hekhalot Rabbati* (section 102, above, p. 19) may be the—only—indication of the "intrusion" of the theology of the name into *Hekhalot Rabbati.*

embedded in a liturgical context whose perfect expression can be viewed as the often-cited response "Blessed be the name of the glory of his kingdom forever and ever." The praise of the name is the single adequate answer to the revelation experienced through the names. In 3 Enoch the names of God are mentioned in one passage only, which furthermore is redactionally problematic. There they are part of the heavenly liturgy and, as such, without relation to man (as is the case particularly in *Maʿaseh Merkavah* and *Merkavah Rabbah,* but also in *Hekhalot Zuṭarti*).

Only in *Merkavah Rabbah* is the tradition of the immeasurable dimensions of the divine stature (*Shiʿur Qomah*) a prominent element of the macroform. It consists of both measurements and names, whereby the names, so to speak, are the "efficacy" of God in the world, the way in which he makes himself known to man.

In *Hekhalot Zuṭarti* alone the question is posed, and in an unusually exacerbated manner, whether one can see God. The answer is given in a threefold form: (a) the "vision" of God consists of the communication of his names; (b) ʿAqiva says he looks like us but is concealed from us; (c) Moses says it is not decisive to see him or whether one can see him, but rather to praise him. The text undoubtedly wishes, in its elaborate redactional composition, to state that God revealed himself through ʿAqiva (and only through ʿAqiva) and that this revelation consists of his names.

Angels

In no other macroform are the angels the central theme as in 3 Enoch. Only here is a systematized angelology (whereby an attempt is made to combine various systems) and a comprehensive hierarchy to be found. Enoch, who has been transformed into Meṭaṭron, stands at the head of all the angels; as "lesser YHWH" he is the representative of God, endowed with the same attributes and, like God, omniscient. The main task of the angels (not of Meṭaṭron) is the praise of God, which is carried out chiefly in the *Qedushah* and takes place without reference to man. The divine liturgy is at best (in the surrounding narrative frame) the model for the earthly liturgy.

In contrast to 3 Enoch, *Hekhalot Rabbati* contains no systematic angelology, although the angels do play a thoroughly important and manifold role. On the one hand, they are the bearers of the divine throne and those whose most distinguished task is praising—with the *Qedushah*—God. As such, they live, with the *ḥayyot ha-qodesh* at their head, in perfect harmony with God; in particular, the *ḥayyot ha-qodesh* are consumed with a longing for God. On the other hand, their dominant function, especially in *Hekhalot Rabbati,* is as gatekeepers at the entrances to the seven *hekhalot,* to whom the *yored merkavah* must show the magic seals to pass by unhindered. Meṭaṭron's importance is completely subordinate in *Hekhalot Rabbati.* We learn instead, amongst other things, of an "angel of the countenance" as the highest master of ceremonies and of ʿAnafiʾel, who as keeper of the divine signet ring and guardian at the entrance to the seventh *hekhal* is almost equal to God. Finally, in the clearly defined *sar ha-torah* unit there reigns the "Prince of the Torah" (Yofiʾel) who helps toward the acquisition of complete knowledge of the Torah.

In all other macroforms the angels are of rather lesser significance. Analogous to the different conception of God in the various redactional layers, *Hekhalot Zuṭarti* also exhibits two different valuations in the theology of the angels. In one layer, the concern is almost exclusively with the *ḥayyot ha-qodesh,* who are simultaneously very close to and very far away from God (because despite their direct proximity to the throne, they are unable to see him—in contrast to man, i.e., ʿAqiva). In the other layer, the angels function mainly as guardian angels at the entrances to the *hekhalot* and examiners of the *yored merkavah;* and thus they are closely related to the angels in *Hekhalot Rabbati.*

In contrast to *Hekhalot Rabbati* and *Zuṭarti,* the guardian angels in *Maʿaseh Merkavah* and *Merkavah Rabbah* are either completely absent (*Merkavah Rabbah*) or appear only rarely (*Maʿaseh Merkavah*). In both macroforms they are primarily those who transmit the revelation (of the Torah), whereby this revelation takes place on earth and is connected mostly with the knowledge of the names (of God and the angels). Their foremost task remains the praise of God; however, this praise does not culminate in the *Qedushah* (as in 3 Enoch and *Hekhalot Rabbati*), but consists of the divine names. Meṭaṭron as well (whose names together with that of God flow into one another) aids man in obtaining knowledge of the Torah.

Man

The relationship of man to the heavenly world moves in all of the analyzed macroforms between the two poles of the "heavenly journey" (i.e., the "descent" to the throne of glory), on the one hand, and the magical-theurgic "act of adjuration," on the other. Between these two poles is a wide spectrum of in part different, in part intertwined units of tradition, which must be comprehended in its complexity without prematurely becoming pinned down in the respective extreme possibilities.

Heavenly Journey. The macroform of the heavenly journey par excellence is *Hekhalot Rabbati.* After the exact analysis one can even state that the form of the heavenly journey, which since Scholem normally has been allotted the center of the Hekhalot literature, is found *only* in *Hekhalot Rabbati.* There, the classical heavenly journey of the *yored merkavah* (in several arrangements) is described, with the examination of the adept, the knowledge of the Torah as entrance ticket, and the display of seals; there, God longingly awaits the adept, and (only) there, the *yored merkavah* is praised in messianic tones, as it were, as the chosen one of Israel. There, the *yored merkavah* is Israel's emissary, who by his heavenly journey constitutes anew the communion between God and Israel and sees to it that it can be realized continually in the liturgy. The *yored merkavah* guarantees God's love for Israel and delivers the message that Israel therein is superior to the angels, even to God's privileged *ḥayyot.*

This form of the heavenly journey indeed is to be found in other macroforms, however, with notable differences. In 3 Enoch it is reduced to the opening sentence of the narrative frame; in the other texts, the characteristics of the classical form of *Hekhalot Rabbati* are absent either entirely or for the most part (*Maʿaseh Merkavah; Merkavah Rabbah*). *Hekhalot Zuṭarti* alone, in the redactional layer of sections 407–426, transmits very similar traditions of ascent, known to us from *Hekhalot Rabbati* (guardian angels, seals, examination, vision, praise of God as king). Nevertheless, the report of ascent at the end of *Hekhalot Zuṭarti* is imbued with a very specific coloration, which substantially differentiates it from *Hekhalot Rabbati:* it culminates in an adjuration and thus receives a theurgic component that for the most part is alien to the heavenly journey in *Hekhalot Rabbati.* The same is true of ʿAqiva's heavenly journey at the end of *Merkavah Rabbah,* where the ascent itself is reduced to a short sentence and in which the vision of God flows into the demand to adjure Meṭaṭron for the sake of the study of the Torah.

Adjuration. Before I consider further forms of the combination of the "heavenly journey" and the "adjuration," the other pole of the spectrum must be examined more precisely. The notion of the "adjuration" stands as an abridgement for what normally is termed the *sar ha-torah* traditions in the literature (although the "Prince of the Torah" is rarely mentioned). All of these traditions share the performance of magical-theurgic acts of adjuration to obtain command of the Torah.

The classical formulation of this unit of tradition is the Torah myth in *Hekhalot Rabbati:* Israel takes possession of the Torah against the opposition of the angels, although not through the traditional way of learning, but with the aid of magic. The implementation of magic guarantees the complete knowledge of the Torah, and this is equivalent to earthly power (i.e., in this world and not only in the world to come). One who possesses the Torah in its entirety determines the "order of the world" and is lord not only over earth, but over heaven as well.

The Torah myth, as described in the unique and highly poetic form of *Hekhalot Rabbati,* can be seen as the foundation for the second formulation of the *sar ha-torah* unit, the adjuration of an angel. A large number of various forms can be observed here; however, the aim of all of them is the same: the point is always the command of the Torah and precisely how one can protect oneself from forgetting it. Preparatory practices such as fasting, sexual abstinence, and ritual baths often precede the adjuration.[3] The following elements are structural components of the adjuration:

1. The angel "binds" himself to man so that he can "adjure" him and "use" him. The formal language of the adjuration formulas is very specific and manifold[4] and witnessed in almost all macroforms (seldom in *Hekhalot Zuṭarti* and not at all in 3 Enoch).

2. In a singular unit of tradition, which is transmitted in both *Hekhalot Rabbati* and *Merkavah Rabbah,* the adjuration does not occur through the medium of an angel but directly from man to man: R. Neḥunyah b. Haqanah adjures R. Yishmaʿel directly with the "great seal" and the "great oath." Here as well, the result is that he no longer forgets the Torah.

3. In nearly all of the adjurations, the names of God and the angels (and sometimes also seals, which, however, likewise consist of

---

[3]Cf. above, pp. 53, 90, 93; and in detail Gruenwald, *Apocalyptic and Merkavah Mysticism,* pp. 99ff.

[4]See Schäfer, *Hekhalot-Studien,* pp. 258ff.

names) play a major role. This is especially true of *Maʿaseh Merkavah* and *Merkavah Rabbah*. The theurgic use of the names can be independent of the adjuration of a specific angel, as above all in the macroform *Merkavah Rabbah*. This macroform revolves around the "mystery" of the names of God and the angels, the knowledge of which brings about the command of the Torah. Here the names, to a certain degree, are independent of their bearers and have become directly accessible to the Merkavah mystic. This is particularly evident in the magical actions described in *Merkavah Rabbah:* one writes the names of God on leaves and fingernails and then puts these in the mouth to erase them with saliva and thus incorporate them; or one writes the names on a bowl and erases them with wine (which then undoubtedly is drunk). Similar practices are transmitted in *Maʿaseh Merkavah,* although there the magical acts are still connected to the adjuration of angels.

4. Finally, prayer can be a means of adjuration, in various ways combined with names and magical actions. This form of adjuration is particularly characteristic of *Maʿaseh Merkavah,* but can be found as well in *Merkavah Rabbah*. More apparent than in the other adjuration texts, it is embedded in a ritual-liturgical context, which however clearly is related to the individual and not the community.

Combined Forms. In view of the finding that a "pure" heavenly journey is very rare and magical adjuration is by far the more prevalent, the "combined forms" between the two are of particular interest. Besides the aforementioned texts in which a heavenly journey culminates in adjuration,[5] two further forms of the combination in *Hekhalot Zuṭarti* and in *Maʿaseh Merkavah* are significant here.

In the redactional layer of sections 335–374 of *Hekhalot Zuṭarti,* Moses' heavenly journey does not transmit the Torah in the traditional sense, but precisely the knowledge of the names with whose help one can protect oneself from forgetting the Torah. Accordingly, ʿAqiva's ascent in the framework of the *pardes* story (a prototype of the heavenly journey!) is interpreted, or reinterpreted, through the redactional embedment in the context of the magical usage of the names: the ascent of ʿAqiva, who alone returned unharmed from the *pardes,* also served the purpose of "fetching" the name or names of God, which "hold together" heaven and earth,

---

[5] See above, p. 143.

and making them known to man. The redactor of *Hekhalot Zuṭarti* thus related most radically the ascent traditions to his central theme, the theology of the divine name.[6] It is not per chance that *Hekhalot Zuṭarti* is the macroform in which the danger stemming from the names (cf. the danger of the heavenly journey) and their further transmission is stressed most emphatically and in which the theurgic potency and the cosmic power of the names are expressed most poetically.

In the same manner as the prayer in *Maʿaseh Merkavah* can serve as a means of the magical adjuration, it can also cause the ascent and simultaneously (amongst other things) be an element of the object viewed as well as the result of the vision. The place of the actual ascent, which is so extensively described in *Hekhalot Rabbati,* has been occupied by prayer; the ascent, so to speak, is transformed into prayer. The ascent undoubtedly also receives a magical dimension through the strong magical component of the prayer in *Maʿaseh Merkavah.*

The Protagonists of the Heavenly Journey and the Adjuration. If we inquire summarily into the actor of the heavenly journey and the adjuration, we find that the macroforms place quite different emphases. The *yored merkavah* in *Hekhalot Rabbati* is the chosen one of Israel, who as such represents Israel, though he surely is not arbitrarily interchangeable. Characteristic of this tendency is also the so-called *ḥavurah* report, in which the rabbi's "fellowship" is introduced to the mysteries of the Merkavah.[7] In a somewhat tense relation to this stands the passage in which it is explicitly stressed that "anyone" who is free from idolatry, lewdness, bloodshed, slander, false oath, profanation of the (divine) name, impudence, and baseless animosity, and who observes all of the commands and prohibitions, can erect a ladder in his house and "descend" to the Merkavah.[8] This displays that, also within the traditions of ascent in *Hekhalot Rabbati,* various trends and tendencies have been processed. The subject of the adjuration in the *sar ha-torah* traditions in addition to R. Yishmaʿel is "every man."

In contrast to this, *Hekhalot Zuṭarti* provides a different view. Here the ascent (in the sections 335–374) is limited to Moses and

---

[6] Cf. also sections 420–424 where traditions of ascent and adjuration likewise are closely connected.

[7] Sections 198ff. (*Hekhalot Rabbati*).

[8] Sections 199f.

R. ʿAqiva; they make the names that they bring from their ascent accessible to their students, and thus to a circle of initiates. Suitable to this is the warning against the further distribution of the received "mystery," which points to the esoteric knowledge of a closed group.

In *Maʿaseh Merkavah* as well, the protagonists of the heavenly journey are heroes of the past (ʿAqiva and Neḥunyah ben Haqanah); however, their experiences are transmitted through R. Yishmaʿel, and there is left no doubt that "anyone" can imitate them. This is even more true of the magical adjuration in which Yishmaʿel only serves as the role model for "anyone" who (preferably in prayer) adjures the angel and desires to obtain knowledge of the Torah.

Most consistent in this tendency is *Merkavah Rabbah* (which thus adopts the extreme opposite position to parts of *Hekhalot Rabbati* and *Zuṭarti*) with its reinterpretation of the chain of tradition of *Pirqe Avot,* which alludes to the rabbis, to "all of Israel," and with its inclusion of the proselyte in the circle of those to whom Meṭaṭron "binds himself," thus those who can successfully adjure an angel. It perhaps is no accident that this most comprehensive and open position is to be found in connection with the adjuration tradition[9] and not the heavenly journey. Nonetheless, one must be cautious with generalized conclusions, as *Hekhalot Rabbati* also displays quite contrary tendencies and even the opposite position in *Hekhalot Zuṭarti* belongs to the broader context of the adjuration.[10]

3 Enoch. Also with regard to the relationship between man and the heavenly world, 3 Enoch differs greatly from the other macroforms. The central theme indeed is the heavenly journey, although not in the style of the Hekhalot literature but rather in that of the classical apocalypse: with an *angelus interpres* (Meṭaṭron) as guide through the heavenly geography, and R. Yishmaʿel as the one being led. At the end is salvation for Israel and the individual in the traditional style, whereby the standards of early Jewish and rabbinic anthropology (reward and punishment) dominate. Only one Genizah fragment turns this basic tendency of the "classical" 3 Enoch upside down and has man's fate predestined; that is, dependent on astrological constellations. The fact that this Genizah

---

[9] More precisely, with an adjuration integrated into a heavenly journey; see above, pp. 118f.

[10] Which likewise is transmitted through a heavenly journey; above, pp. 67f.

fragment represents an earlier stage of the manuscript tradition is uncontested; however, the question whether it reflects an earlier stage of the macroform 3 Enoch finally cannot be answered, due to the scanty evidence of the manuscripts. In any case, the Genizah fragment is nearer the magical "core" of the Hekhalot literature than the classical form of 3 Enoch, which displays close similarities with the apocalyptic and rabbinic literature. If the Genizah fragment represents an earlier stage of the macroform 3 Enoch, and there is much that supports this theory, this would mean that in later manuscripts that represent the classical 3 Enoch, a rerabbinizing of originally stronger astrological-magical traditions took place.

The Hidden and Manifest God

The thematic spectrum covered by the terms *God, angel,* and *man* certainly is central to the Hekhalot literature, although it is not comprehensive enough to deal with all of the important themes. Nevertheless, it is worthwhile, in light of the attained results, to inquire into some of the questions posed by contemporary research on early Jewish mysticism.

Transcendence and Immanence

As we have seen, the king seated on his throne is for Gershom Scholem the center of the Hekhalot literature, and he characterizes early Jewish mysticism as cosmocratorial mysticism and (following the example of Graetz) "Basileomorphism": the God of Merkavah mysticism is the God of transcendence and not the God of immanence.

The central importance of the theology of the throne and that of the king in the Hekhalot literature and particularly in *Hekhalot Rabbati* cannot be denied; and it would be wrong to ignore this fact one-sidedly against Scholem. It is equally misguided, however, to single out the aspect of God's kingdom and his transcendence and turn it into the all-dominant theme. Yet it seems to me, that Scholem succumbed to exactly this danger, a danger that can be brought about by the style and opulent language of the Hekhalot literature (and above all that of *Hekhalot Rabbati*) in ever-new phrases and endless litanies. The purpose of the heavenly journey is precisely to span the spatial distance between heaven and earth, man and God, and to penetrate the transcendence of God on his throne in heaven.

The message of the Hekhalot literature is that this is possible, that the *yored merkavah* as Israel's emissary can reach the divine throne. Notwithstanding the emphasis on the danger connected with the ascent, the texts leave no doubt that God passionately desires this ascent above all else. The power of the angels, who attempt to prevent the ascent, in reality is limited. Despite the spatial distance between God and Israel, which the *yored merkavah* alone can span, either physically or psychically, Israel is closer to God than the angels and, in reality, God's love is meant for his people, Israel. God's transcendence, as the king who reigns in remote heavens, is dissolved by his love of man and Israel and is transformed into an immanence, which in some respects is of a more intimate nature than the immanence known to us from traditional rabbinic literature. The competition for God's love is won by Israel, not by the angels and not by the *ḥayyot ha-qodesh,* who are self-consumed by their, in the end, unanswered devotion.

The only angel in 3 Enoch and several layers of the other macroforms who constitutes an exception and is so close to God as to be dressed in similar clothes and sit on a similar throne is Meṭaṭron, the "lesser YHWH." This Meṭaṭron, however, is precisely not an angel like the others but the man Enoch transformed into an angel. Enoch-Meṭaṭron, as the prototype of the *yored merkavah,* shows that man can come very close to God, so close as to be almost similar to him, so that Aher-Elishaʿ ben ʿAvuyah can mistake him for God[11] and only one missing letter distinguishes his name from that of God.

The *Shiʿur Qomah* traditions also provide a very differentiated answer to the question of God's transcendence and immanence. It is correct, as D. Halperin has noted,[12] that their attempt to establish the measurements of the divine limbs in analogy to the human body is marked by a crass anthropomorphism (which becomes even more clear when one compares it to the corresponding passages of the Targum to Ezekiel 1:27). However, this is only partially true. First, not all of the measurements in all of the *Shiʿur Qomah* units can be reconciled with the dimensions of the human body. Second, and this is of greater importance, the *Shiʿur Qomah* tradition does not intend to state that God can be "calculated," that he is, so to speak, a superman of enormous yet exactly measurable and conceivable dimensions. The point of the completely absurd calculations is to

---

[11]See above, p. 133, n. 53.

[12]*The Faces of the Chariot,* pp. 405ff.

demonstrate that God cannot be conceived of in human categories: he, "as it were," is like a human being and yet hidden. God's immanence is not a result of the measurements of his limbs and his likeness to man, but rather a result of his names that are communicated as well. The names establish the relationship between God and man, and God reveals himself in his names to man, who uses them and by which he can rule the world and, in the end, God as well. God is transcendent *and* immanent, at the same time hidden *and* revealed.

The same ambivalence also is displayed by the other line of tradition in the Hekhalot literature, the adjuration. By allowing man to adjure the angels, the hidden God places himself under his power. "The servants are adjured through their master": the most significant element of this adjuration are the names, whereby, as we have seen, the names of God and his angels often are inseparable. Through the knowledge and use of the names in the adjuration (and the heavenly journey that is combined with the adjuration), man gains power over God and his angels. That the purpose of the adjuration lies in the complete mastering of the Torah, certainly implies *as well* that man thereby hopes to be able to achieve the comprehensive fulfillment of the commandments, although surely not this alone. The Torah consists not only of commandments but in a deeper, and in later mysticism a self-evident sense, of letters and names. He who "possesses" the Torah in its entirety is ruler of the world, the order of the cosmos, and thereby of God as well. Through the names revealed by God, man has God at his disposal, as a result he has been given precisely the means by which he becomes master of the earth and heaven.

Ecstatic Heavenly Journey and Magical-Theurgic Adjuration

As the analysis of the sources has shown, the Hekhalot literature moves between the two poles of the heavenly journey and the magical-theurgic adjuration. This point has been agreed upon by scholars; however, what remains controversial is how this relationship is to be determined more exactly and where the emphases should be placed. Related to this are the elementary questions concerning the dating of both tendencies as well as their original *Sitz im Leben:* do unique ecstatic experiences underlie Merkavah mysticism or is it an expression of a "magic ritual" not necessarily connected with ecstatic practices?

Scholem's answer to this question is unequivocal (and most of his successors have adopted his view): the transcendence of God-king corresponds to the ecstatic adventure of man's heavenly journey. In other words, just as God as transcendent king on his throne permeates the conception of God within the Hekhalot literature, so is the heavenly journey the dominant factor in the relationship between man and God. In the spectrum characterized by the two poles "heavenly journey" and "adjuration," the heavenly journey clearly enjoys superiority. This is true in regard to both content and time: the more "heavenly journey," the more original and earlier; the more "adjuration" and *śar ha-torah,* the more secondary and later.[13]

This one-sided view of the Hekhalot literature cannot be maintained. The pure form of the heavenly journey, by which Scholem interprets the entire Hekhalot literature, as we have seen, is very rare; the various forms of the adjuration and the combined forms of the heavenly journey and the adjuration by far are more dominant. As a result, Halperin recently undertook the attempt to define a position opposite to that of Scholem. He does not wish to stop at the obvious finding that the heavenly journey and the adjuration are to be phenomenologically separated from one another and that the adjuration must be elevated to its proper place against the heavenly journey so excessively accentuated by Scholem;[14] he desires to go a decisive step further and explain now, as it were, the heavenly journey through the adjuration (the *śar ha-torah* traditions). Although both traditions are to be separated, they are closely connected to one

---

[13]*Jewish Gnosticism,* pp. 12f.; cf. also Gruenwald, *Apocalyptic and Merkavah Mysticism,* p. 143; idem., *From Apocalypticism to Gnosticism,* pp. 184ff.; J. Dan, "Three Types of Ancient Jewish Mysticism," Seventh Annual Rabbi Louis Feinberg Memorial Lecture in Judaic Studies, University of Cincinnati, 1984, pp. 24ff. Scholem does concede that the heavenly journey also can contain magical elements, but on the whole is inclined to the hypothesis that the adjuration of the *sar ha-torah* is to be separated from the heavenly journey and belongs to a later period, "when the ecstatic ascent had already lost much of its freshness and had been superseded by a greater stress on the magical elements" (ibid., p. 12). In clear contrast to this later dating of the magical traditions is his attempt to show precisely *Hekhalot Zuṭarti* as the oldest text of the Hekhalot literature (*Jewish Gnosticism,* p. 76; *Major Trends of Jewish Mysticism,* p. 45). Therefore, he is forced to differentiate between two layers of magical transmission, one of which belongs to an earlier, the other to a later stage of the Hekhalot literature (*Jewish Gnosticism,* p. 13); although he fails to pursue this. The degree of his ambivalent and contradictory attitude toward magic in the Hekhalot literature is displayed in his (earlier) statements in *Major Trends in Jewish Mysticism,* p. 51. Here the magical elements especially in *Hekhalot Zuṭarti* "far from being later additions or signs of spiritual decadence . . . , belong to the very core of their particular religious system." There can be no doubt, nonetheless, that Scholem's view and representation of Merkavah mysticism is entirely dominated by the heavenly journey.

[14]*The Faces of the Chariot,* p. 384.

another in their aim and intention. This results, he argues, first from the obvious combination of heavenly journey and *śar ha-torah* traditions; second however, and this is his most forceful argument, he believes that he found the link between the two in the midrashic traditions of Moses' ascent to Sinai: "I now propose that these Sinai-ascension *haggadot* provide the model both for the *Hekhalot's* trance-journey material and for *Śar Torah.* They form a framework inside which the trance-journey and *Śar Torah* fit together, and each becomes comprehensible in the light of the other."[15] In other words, the goal of the heavenly journey also is the bringing down of the Torah for magical use: "More specifically, I suggest that certain people, nurtured on the stories of how Moses climbed to heaven and seized Torah from the angels, used these images to express and to satisfy their own yearning to have Torah made accessible to them. They imagined more recent heroes, Ishmael and Akiba and Nehuniah b. ha-Qanah, replicating Moses' feat, and then making the results available to others through magical technique."[16]

Here the (simplified representation) of Scholem's position indeed is turned upside down and the adjuration not only is declared the epicenter of the Hekhalot literature, but the *entire* Hekhalot literature is interpreted exclusively through the adjuration. To begin with, methodologically this is no less problematic than Scholem's interpretation; in place of the pure form of the heavenly journey, the adjuration and its combination with the heavenly journey has been elevated to the pivotal position of the interpretation of the Hekhalot literature and thereby to its focal point. Both approaches suffer from the desire to find *one* explanation for the *entire* Hekhalot literature, which then assigns all other parts to their places, thus ignoring the extremely complex relations of the texts and the various literary layers within the individual macroforms. The Hekhalot literature is not a unity and, therefore, cannot be explained uniformly.

Halperin's interpretation also is inconclusive with regard to the contents. The idea that the visions of the heavenly journey of the Hekhalot mystics are inspired by the Sinai exegeses of synagogue liturgy is little more than a postulate; definitive evidence within the Hekhalot literature remains very vague. And above all, the pure form of the heavenly journey, which despite its rarity cannot be simply ignored, nowhere has as its purpose the transmission of the To-

---

[15]Ibid., p. 385.
[16]Ibid.

rah. On the contrary, the most important quality the *yored merkavah* must bring with him besides his magic seals to successfully pass the guardian angels at the gates of the seven *hekhalot* is the knowledge of the Torah, which, so to speak, is the entrance ticket pinned to the wagon that takes him to the seventh *hekhal.* The *yored merkavah* of *Hekhalot Rabbati,* the prototype of the "pure" heavenly journey, does not receive the Torah in the seventh *hekhal,* he brings it with him.

Finally, it is of no use to belittle the declared aim of this form of heavenly journey, the vision of the king in his beauty, by the question "why anyone should want to do *that?*"[17] The information the texts provide concerning what the successful *yored merkavah* actually sees indeed is disappointing, but this does not yet justify placing the heavenly journey completely under the guardianship of the *sar hatorah* traditions because these are easier to comprehend.[18] The *yored merkavah* beholds God in his beauty and sees what "occurs" on God's countenance[19]—the fact that we are told almost nothing about the contents of what he sees does not mean that he sees nothing and instead receives the Torah. The type of heavenly journey represented (mainly) by *Hekhalot Rabbati* must remain a peculiar and legitimate offspring of the Hekhalot literature alongside the (surely overwhelming) unit of the magical-theurgic adjuration.

However, the question as to the ecstatic character of the heavenly journey has not yet been answered. Halperin correctly pointed out that Scholem's view of the Hekhalot literature is to a certain degree inspired by a joint responsum of the Babylonian scholars Sherira and Hai Gaon (ca. 1000 C.E.), in which a causal connection between magical practices and the ecstatic heavenly journey is stated:[20]

> Remember that many scholars were of the belief that one in possession of certain explicitly defined qualities, who

[17]Ibid., p. 370. The rationalistic argumentation has here sprouted strange buds.

[18]Cf. ibid., p. 384.

[19]Vision and liturgy obviously belong close together, and it thus would be wrong to ignore the visual element in the Hekhalot literature; it is equally wrong, however, to portray the vision of God as the apparent main goal of the Merkavah mystic, as opposed to the liturgy (Gruenwald, *From Apocalypticism to Gnosticism,* p. 184). See above, p. 18, and pp. 164f.

[20]Scholem, *Major Trends in Jewish Mysticism,* p. 49; Halperin, "A New Edition of Hekhalot Literature," *JAOS* 104 (1984): 549ff.; *The Faces of the Chariot,* pp. 6, 360, 374; cf. also Schäfer, *Hekhalot-Studien,* p. 284.

desires to behold the Merkavah and the palaces [*hekhalot*] of the angels on high, must follow certain procedures. He must fast a certain number of days, put his head between his knees and whisper many traditional songs and hymns to the earth. Then he gazes into their[21] inner rooms and chambers, as if seeing the seven palaces with his own eyes, and he sees, as if entering from one palace into the other, and perceives what is in it.[22] There are two Mishnayot which the Tannaites teach in this matter, and they are called *Hekhalot Rabbati* and *Hekhalot Zuṭarti*.[23]

The only passage in the Hekhalot literature, as Halperin also pointed out,[24] to which the responsum may refer, is found in *Hekhalot Zuṭarti*:[25]

R. ʿAqiva said:
Everyone who repeats [= learns] this Mishnah
and wishes to expressly utter the name [of God]
must fast for forty days.
He must put his head between his knees
until the fast has taken complete hold of him
and whisper to the earth and not to heaven,
so that the earth will hear and not heaven.

This passage indeed belongs in the broader connection of one of ʿAqiva's heavenly journeys, but it is clear from the context that the concern here is not a heavenly journey but the magical use of the name of God, thus an adjuration. If *Hekhalot Zuṭarti* was the source of the responsum, then the connection between magical practice and heavenly journey was established by the responsum and not by *Hekhalot Zuṭarti*. The adept who is instructed by ʿAqiva does not enter into a state of ecstatic rapture that transfers him either psychically or even physically to the seventh *hekhal*, but at most falls into a trance

[21]'The palaces'.

[22]Each indiviual palace.

[23]B. M. Lewin, *Otzar ha-Geonim*, vol. 4/2 (Ḥagiga), part 1 (Teshuvot), p. 14; cf. also p. 61.

[24]*The Faces of the Chariot*, p. 374.

[25]Section 424.

and thereby is able, without incurring injury to himself or his environment, to utter the ineffable name of God; that is, to use the magical power of the divine name.[26]

The Hekhalot literature does not provide us any indication as to *how* the heavenly journey actually is carried out, or even *if* it is practiced at all as a "truly" ecstatic experience. It appears as though Scholem's interpretation is inspired by the model of a gnostic heavenly journey of the soul, which itself and with regard to its alleged influence on the Hekhalot literature is questionable.[27] Where the heavenly journey and the adjuration are connected to one another, the magical-theurgic element is so strong as to raise valid doubts concerning a practice of the heavenly journey (regardless of its form). However, even the classical paradigm of the heavenly journey in *Hekhalot Rabbati* remains silent as to how the adept manages to enter into the state of the *yored merkavah* and whether he experiences the heavenly journey as a psychical or physical adventure. The text begins without any further explanation with the sentence: "Which are the hymns that are said by the one who wishes to behold the vision of the Merkavah and to descend and ascend unharmed?"[28] These hymns surely are not songs intended to transfer the Merkavah mystic into a state of trance and ecstasy, but rather the *Qedushah* songs extensively described later on and all revolve around the trishagion of Isaiah 6:3. This points to a definite liturgical *Sitz im Leben* of the heavenly journey, which does not necessarily exclude ecstatic implications, but makes them relatively unlikely. The fact that the adjuration traditions also often are embedded in a liturgical context (prayer, learning the Midrash)[29] lends support to the claim that the heavenly journey and the adjuration were understood as ritual-liturgical actions.[30] The point of departure in both cases is the same (the synagogue or the private prayer on earth), only the goal is different: in the heavenly journey, man "meets" God in heaven; in the

[26]Halperin, *The Faces of the Chariot,* pp. 374f.: "Akiba's visiting the *merkabah* is important for him, not because he is necessarily going to imitate it, but because it has opened channels of power from which he can now profit."

[27]Scholem, *Major Trends in Jewish Mysticism,* pp. 49ff.; see the criticism of Gruenwald, *Apocalyptic and Merkavah Mysticism,* pp. 110ff.; idem., *From Apocalypticism to Gnosticism,* pp. 191ff., and of P. S. Alexander, "Comparing Merkavah Mysticism and Gnosticism. An Essay in Method," *JJS* 35 (1984): 1–18.

[28]Section 81.

[29]Cf. above, pp. 36, 95, 111ff.; and *Hekhalot-Studien,* p. 294.

[30]Cf. now also Janowitz, *The Poetics of Ascent,* in particular pp. 97ff.

adjuration they meet on the earth. The common element of both is magic, which, in different ways to be sure (according to the various macroforms and the various literary layers within them), permeates the heavenly journey and the adjuration.

Finally, what does this mean concerning the question of dating the two poles heavenly journey and adjuration? In opposition to Scholem, Halperin now wishes to see the adjuration as not only possessing conceptual but also temporal priority: "But I can see nothing in the texts to support the idea that passages speaking of heavenly ascent are older than the *Śar Torah* materials. This view seems to rest mainly on the prejudice that whatever sounds more purely 'mystical' must be more authentic, and therefore earlier."[31] This conclusion certainly is correct, as it is obvious that Scholem worked with a very contradictory notion of "original" = "early" and "degenerate" (magic!) = "late."[32] However, Halperin's further argument is thereby not necessarily convincing: "On the contrary, the *Śar Torah* incantations have a claim to priority in that their purpose, unlike that of the trance-journey, is basically intelligible."[33] Here again, Scholem is simply turned upside down, and based on the supposed conceptual priority of the adjuration traditions, their temporal priority is deduced; the one is just as inconclusive as the other.

If one adopts the sequence of the analyzed macroforms—*Hekhalot Rabbati, Hekhalot Zuṭarti, Maᶜaseh Merkavah, Merkavah Rabbah,* 3 Enoch—then a clear tendency becomes obvious: from the "pure" form of the heavenly journey in *Hekhalot Rabbati* over various combined forms (in various shades) to the overwhelming domination of the adjuration in *Merkavah Rabbah* (3 Enoch as a special case is not taken into account here).[34] However, this tendency stands and falls with the postulated sequence of the macroforms, which remains very tentative.[35] We neither know enough about the relations

---

[31]*The Faces of the Chariot,* p. 384.

[32]See above, p. 151, n. 13.

[33]Ibid.

[34]It is not per chance that precisely *Merkavah Rabbah* is the key to Halperin's understanding of the heavenly journey: "It is not easy to see why anyone would care about 'descent to the merkavah'; unless, as *Merkavah Rabbah* suggests, he saw in this journey a source and legitimation for *Sar Torah.*"

[35]Nevertheless, there is some reason to believe that at least the redactional layer of sections 407–426 in *Hekhalot Zuṭarti* is dependent on *Hekhalot Rabbati* and not the other way around (above, pp. 61, 73, 74) and that the ascent traditions in *Maᶜaseh Merkavah* (above, p. 83), in *Merkavah Rabbah* (above, p. 99, n. 45, pp. 102, 112ff.)

of the macroforms to one another, nor (far less) is the critical literary and redactional deciphering of the macroforms advanced enough to allow us to provide precise information concerning the temporal relation between the heavenly journey and the magical-theurgic adjuration. Both must (temporarily) remain beside one another and neither through literary (sequence of the "writings") nor imaginary maneuvers (the ecstatic heavenly journey is "more original,"—the adjuration is "more intelligible") can they be set in a temporal succession.

Esoteric and Exoteric

The Hekhalot literature leaves us fully in the dark as to who its authors were and which circles we might assume were the bearers and creators of the ideas contained within it. Concerning this question we also find two opposing positions. Whereas Scholem rather self-evidently[36] started with the assumption that the traditions of the esoteric "discipline" *maʿaseh merkavah,* which are vaguely alluded to and only fragmentarily preserved in rabbinic literature, are brought to light in their entirety and originality in the Hekhalot literature, Halperin raises doubts about the connection between rabbinic *maʿaseh merkavah* and Hekhalot literature, and as a result sees no reason for an esoteric understanding of the Hekhalot literature.

Here as well, a generalized conclusion has been drawn from a correct premise. The analyzed macroforms exhibit a quite ambivalent picture,[37] there indeed is a *tendency* to emphasize that anyone can partake of the experience transmitted by the heavenly journey and the adjuration. This, however, is only a tendency, which in the individual macroforms is accentuated in various manners: strongest in *Merkavah Rabbah,* and weakest in *Hekhalot Zuṭarti* with its clear

---

and 3 Enoch (above, p. 135) rather can be seen as a reduction of the "drafts" of *Hekhalot Rabbati.* The special role of 3 Enoch and its traditional and historical placement at the end of the transmission process of the Hekhalot literature also appears to be confirmed. *Maʿaseh Merkavah* and *Merkavah Rabbah* belong so close together in numerous aspects, that it is superfluous to inquire into their exact location within the relative chronology of the macroforms.

[36]And in opposition in particular to Graetz, "Die mystiche Literatur in der gaonischen Epoche," *MGWJ* 8 (1859): 109ff.; Scholem, *Major Trends in Jewish Mysticism,* pp. 61 and 66.

[37]Above, pp. 146f.

stress on the secret teaching.[38] The Hekhalot literature is both esoteric and exoteric. Further progress on this question will be made possible only through more extensive research into its traditional and redactional history and not through own-sided and generalized statements in one or the other direction.

This is true even more so for Halperin's next step. If the Hekhalot literature in principle is not an esoteric discipline, he argues further, but rather for everyone, then this can mean only that "we are not to look for the originators of the *Hekhalot* in any esoteric clique, but among the Jewish masses."[39] Who could these "Jewish masses" be in the context of rabbinic Judaism? None other than the well-known *ʿam ha-ʾareṣ,* who in the Hekhalot literature rebels as the less-privileged lower class against the upper class of the rabbis. The main evidence for this thesis is served by the Torah myth in *Hekhalot Rabbati,* which only on the surface deals with the rivalry between angels and man;[40] in reality it is concerned with the rebellion of the uneducated against the scholars.[41] The means by which this rebellion is brought about is magic.

Here again, *one* aspect of the exceedingly multilayered Hekhalot literature is raised to the key position of the whole. To start with, this is a methodological objection. Furthermore, it remains fully unclear why precisely the Torah myth should be a reflection of the "social conditions" of the rabbis and the *ʿam ha-ʾareṣ.* The Torah myth in *Hekhalot Rabbati* is the adaptation of a widely ramified Midrash tradition;[42] Halperin therefore either must show that already the Midrash does not aim at the rivalry between angels and man, but at the rivalry between the rabbis and the *ʿam ha-ʾareṣ,* or else show both that the Torah myth in *Hekhalot Rabbati* has reinterpreted the Midrash in this sense and how it has done so. The reference to magic alone does not suffice. The decisive difference between the Midrash

---

[38]Halperin, *The Faces of the Chariot,* p. 386, is familiar with the passages in *Hekhalot Zuṭarti,* but he plays down their significance in favor of his uniform view.

[39]*The Faces of the Chariot,* p. 385.

[40]Against my thesis in "Engel und Menschen in der Hekhalot-Literatur," in *Hekhalot-Studien,* pp. 265ff.

[41]"The angels, then, appear as spokesmen for a privileged group whose claim to privilege rests on mastery of the Torah. Who are the 'Israelites' whom God favors against them? They are 'humble folk' . . . , people who are too busy doing manual labor to have time for the Torah. . . . Do we know any Jewish group during the rabbinic period that would fit this description? We do. . . . They are the *ʿam haʾareṣ,* literally 'people of the land'." Halperin, *The Faces of the Chariot,* p. 437.

[42]Cf. *Hekhalot-Studien,* pp. 269ff., 291f.

and the Torah myth indeed lies in the magical acquisition of the Torah ("not through toil and not through labor, but through the name of this seal and through the mention of the crown"),[43] but where are there grounds for arguing that here a conflict between the *ʿam ha-ʾareṣ* and the rabbis is expressed? It appears that Halperin is being led by the (unspoken) premise that magic is exclusively the means of the "humble man" with which he arms himself against the superior power of the "ruling class" of Torah scholars. Research into Jewish magic of late antiquity is still in its infancy and is an urgent desideratum.[44] In any case, it has reached nowhere near the point that one can define groups within rabbinic Judaism and weigh them against one another on the basis of magic. On the contrary, everything points to the fact that all groups within the Judaism of late antiquity were affected by the revolution within the world-view through the penetration of magic, albeit, to be sure, in different ways and to a different extent. The Hekhalot literature is the most comprehensive (though by no means only) attempt to transform the world-view as found in classical rabbinic literature into an increasingly magical conception; to reduce this revolutionary transformation to a shift in power from the rabbis to the *ʿam ha-ʾareṣ* fully disregards the much more differentiated evidence within the Hekhalot literature and thus is not very convincing.

An important argument pertaining to the question of the circles who propagated the ideals of the Hekhalot literature is the pseudepigraphical character of all macroforms.[45] The most important characteristic of the literary genre Hekhalot literature is the great value it places on ascribing itself to certain rabbis, usually to R. Yishmaʿel and R. ʿAqiva. This, to be sure, is not a final proof that the Hekhalot literature in its entirety must be seen as a postrabbinic phenomenon,[46] but there is equally little support for the thesis of a rebellion of the *ʿam ha-ʾareṣ* against the rabbis. Is it plausible that an oppressed lower class would underpin their rebellion against the ruling class precisely by legitimizing themselves with the heroes of this hated caste of scholars? This is surely possible—just as almost

---

[43]Section 289.

[44]Cf. now P. Schäfer, "Jewish Magic Literature in Late Antiquity and Early Middle Ages," *JJS* 41 (1990): 75–91.

[45]Cf. *Hekhalot-Studien*, p. 293.

[46]*Hekhalot-Studien*, ibid.; nonetheless I remain convinced that there is some basis for this supposition.

every paradox is imaginable[47]—although not very likely. The result thus (temporarily?) can be only a very modest one. We do not know who the authors and redactors of the Hekhalot literature were. If they belonged to rabbinic times (which has yet to be proven) then they could just as well have formed a group inside as outside the class of the rabbis; if they belonged to posttalmudic times, then the question concerning their affiliation to the rabbis is irrelevant and their social location even more difficult to determine.

The same reservations finally also must be upheld concerning the question of the geographic location. Whereby Scholem connected his early dating of the Hekhalot literature with its undisputed Palestinian origin,[48] an increasing number of voices now argue that at least the redaction, if not even the origins of parts of the Hekhalot literature, is to be found in Babylonia.[49] Direct indications of this may be the "wise from the house of the master in Babylonia"[50] as well as the difficult text in section 305, in which apparently the use of Torah magic practiced in Babylonia is to be legitimized by the authority of the Palestinian court of law; the use of the term *yeshivah* in *Hekhalot Rabbati*[51] and the custom of the daily recital of the *Qedushah*[52] have been seen indirectly as pointing to a possible Babylonian origin or redaction of *Hekhalot Rabbati*.

This question, too, cannot be answered exclusively in one or the other direction. One will have to reckon more strongly with Babylonian elements and, furthermore, both from a geographic and

---

[47]One, of course, could view it as being a particularly cunning tactical move, which, however, would make sense only if we are dealing with a phenomenon that did not occur simultaneously: over a larger span of time one may have found legitimacy also through the reference to the main representatives of the opponents. The hypothesis of a revolt of the masses against the ruling class of rabbis presumes the same point in time, however.

[48]Cf. more extensively *Übersetzung der Hekhalot-Literatur*, vol. 2, pp. xxiiiff.

[49]Gruenwald, Shirat ha-mal'akhim, p. 474, but see p. 475; J. Dan, "Livʿayyat ha-periodizaṣiyah shel torat ha-sod ha-ʿivrit mi-shilhe ha-ʿet ha-ʿatiqah el yeme-ha-benayyim," Proceedings of the Ninth World Congress of Jewish Studies, Jerusalem, 1986, p. 94; *Übersetzung der Hekhalot-Literatur*, vol. 2, p. xxiv; Halperin, *The Faces of the Chariot*, pp. 370, 435ff.

[50]T.-S. K 21.95.C, fol. 2a, lines 13ff. = *Geniza-Fragmente zur Hekhalot-Literatur*, p. 103; Gruenwald, "Qeṭaʿim ḥadashim mi-sifrut ha-hekhalot," *Tarbiz* 38 (1968–69): 355 and n. 7.

[51]Sections 288f.; Halperin, *The Faces of the Chariot*, pp. 435f.

[52]Gruenwald, "Shirat ha-mal'akhim," pp. 473ff.; Halperin, *The Faces of the Chariot*, p. 437.

temporal point of view, assume a longer germination process whose decipherment will depend on the progress of the critical literary, redactional, and traditional analysis. As recent research has shown,[53] we can follow the development of the Hekhalot literature and with it the process of the magical transformation of the rabbinic conception of the world far into the Middle Ages. One of the highlights of this development is the redaction of the Hekhalot literature by the circles of the German-Jewish pietists (*ḥaside ashkenaz*) of the Rhineland in the twelfth and thirteenth centuries.

Conclusion

Over a period of many centuries, the religion of ancient Judaism developed the conviction that the relationship between God and man is determined by the dynamic relation of the one revelation at Sinai to its continuous explication: God revealed himself to man in a unique historical event at Sinai by giving the Torah to Moses. Everything relevant for understanding the world and the relationship between man and God is concentrated in this Torah. The perception of God and the explanation of the world are accomplished exclusively through the Torah, whereby the doctrine of the oral Torah guarantees that both do not become static, but that they develop dynamically in a continual process. At the end of this process, God's final revelation will occur in the time to come, which culminates in the absolute knowledge and perception of the Torah. Therefore, for the classical rabbinic Judaism, the adequate behavior of man toward God in addition to prayer can be only the study of the Torah.

The authors and redactors of the Hekhalot literature rebel against this traditional conception of the world, which was brought forth by a grandiose literary effort. They were not unaware of the merits of prayer and the Torah, of course. The Hekhalot literature is filled with prayers that share great similarities with those of the synagogue liturgy. Furthermore, the *yored merkavah* in *Hekhalot Rabbati* requires proof that he commands the classical disciplines of the study of the Torah to embark on his heavenly journey. Nevertheless, the traditional repertoire is no longer sufficient for them. They no longer are satisfied with gaining access to God solely through the Torah. In the truest sense of the word, they storm heaven and force direct access to God.

---

[53]Cf. *Hekhalot-Studien*, pp. 3ff.

Not only are the means by which one attains access to God and the understanding of the world thereby changed, but the conception of God as well. In rabbinic Judaism, God reveals himself here and now in the Torah and then finally in the time to come. Therefore, God's concealment is implied, at most, by the fact that his revelation through the Torah in the present time can be only incomplete and temporary and that the fullness of the Torah, and with it that of God, first will be perceivable in the time to come. In the Hekhalot literature God is now, *at present,* at the same time both hidden *and* revealed, which means the following:

1. God is hidden *and* revealed. In principle, neither man nor the angels can see God. To begin with, the theme in this gravity is new. In rabbinic literature the question of whether one can see God plays a minor role that above all is connected to the heroic past. That one is unable to see God at the present time and that God (no longer) reveals himself directly to man is more or less self-evident.[54] The Hekhalot literature not only discusses this question anew, but simultaneously holds it in a curious and ambiguous suspense. God indeed is hidden from man and (to be sure) from the angels, and yet he revealed himself to R. ʿAqiva, the prototype of the yored merkavah, "through the working of the Merkavah, in order to fulfill his wish,"[55] thus through the heavenly journey which is connected to an adjuration. ʿAqiva and his followers; that is, the *yorede merkavah* of the Hekhalot literature, enjoy the privilege that God reveals himself to them.

This ambivalence of being "both hidden as well as revealed" also follows from the *Shiʿur Qomah* traditions in the Hekhalot literature. The decisive statement of *Shiʿur Qomah* is that God does, on the one hand, look like a human being; but, on the other hand, he exceeds all human measurements. God's hidden being expresses itself in dimensions that surpass all human categories and, paradoxically, is conceivable in its imperceptibility.

2. God *at present* is hidden and revealed. In the Hekhalot literature, the two-staged revelation of God at Sinai and in the time to come as found in rabbinic Judaism is concentrated in the immediate experiencing by the *yored merkavah* of the simultaneously hidden and

---

[54] Cf. above, p. 57 and n. 14.

[55] Section 421; see above, pp. 59f.

revealed God. For the most part, the Hekhalot literature abandons the expectation of the end of time, the classical repertoire of this world and the world to come, the messianic redemption and the final judgment. The revelation at Sinai does not culminate in the time to come, but in the heavenly journey or the adjuration by the *yored merkavah*. The protagonists of the Hekhalot literature have lost their patience, they no longer wish to bring about the distant goal of God's revelation through the toilsome study of the Torah. They force direct access to God here and now and complete the revelation at Sinai in their presence. The unbearable period of time between the revelation at Sinai and the time to come is abolished: the *yored merkavah* appears before the divine throne and/or places God at his disposal through the act of adjuration.

The means by which the *yored merkavah* attains revelation are no longer exclusively prayer and the study of the Torah, but above all the heavenly journey and the adjuration. However, prayer and the study of the Torah are not completely abandoned and replaced by the heavenly journey and adjuration; quite the contrary, they are naturally integrated into the new conception of the world that, however, is furnished with implications that go far beyond those of traditional understanding.

1. The new function of prayer is especially clear in those macroforms in which prayer is both the means and the goal of the heavenly journey. The *yored merkavah* executes the heavenly journey through prayer to participate in the heavenly liturgy and at the same time transmit this experience to the earthly community. The "pure" form of the heavenly journey (in *Hekhalot Rabbati*) requires knowledge of the Torah and in addition uses magic (seals) to accomplish the ascent without danger; that is, against the opposition of the angels.

2. The classical form of Torah study is transformed into magical adjuration. That which the labor of the daily study of the Torah promised, but (from the viewpoint of the *yorede merkavah*) was either never realized or put off to the distant future, is to be obtained through the one and repeatable act of adjuration. The essential element of this adjuration and to different degrees also the heavenly journey, are the names of God and the angels (which are inseparably intertwined with one another).

Finally, the new means by which the revelation is attained determine the goal and the contents of this revelation as well.

First, the aim of the heavenly journey is not so much the vision of God on his throne, but more so the participation in the cosmic praise. The "stormy" heavenly occurrence reflected on God's countenance is none other than the heavenly liturgy. The liturgy of the angels is a cosmic event in which God participates as a partner. For this purpose (and only this one) he sets himself on the throne of glory and to a certain extent reacts physically to the praise of the angels. If the *yored merkavah* sees anything, it is precisely this: the overwhelming event of the cosmic liturgy and the change it produces in God. The reigning king on the throne of glory is not a participant in a torpid Byzantine court ritual, but the lively partner in an event that takes place between him and the angels.

The *yored merkavah* participates in this heavenly liturgy in both a passive and active manner: to the extent that heaven and earth are spatially separated, the liturgy in heaven is only that of the angels and not that of man; the *yored merkavah* at most can join in the heavenly liturgy.[56] However, to the extent that he returns from his heavenly journey and is expressively commissioned to report on what he saw and heard, as the emissary of the earthly community, he is an active participant in the heavenly occurrence. His heavenly journey serves the purpose of incorporating the earthly community into the heavenly liturgy and thereby turning it into a truly cosmic event, encompassing heaven and earth, angels and man. In certain redactional layers of the Hekhalot literature the latter is even the real meaning and goal of the divine praise: the heavenly liturgy draws its legitimacy solely from the fact that man takes part in it; without the participation of Israel, it remains useless. The simultaneously passive and active role of the *yored merkavah,* therefore, means that, on the one hand, he sees how the heavenly liturgy is performed, but that, on the other hand, he brings along the most important message of Israel's central role in this heavenly liturgy. The fundamental conviction of rabbinic Judaism, that God is primarily the God of Israel and not of the angels, thus undergoes a new and dramatic intensification.

---

[56]Here as well, the differences between the macroforms must be considered. In sections 550f. (*Maʿaseh Merkavah*) the *yored merkavah* = R. ʿAqiva intones a hymn on high, which consists of the synagogal *ʿAlenu* in the individual form of the *ʿAlai:* he is the emissary of the earthly community but says *his* hymn, as he is alone on high.

The *yored merkavah* is the emissary of the earthly community. This implies further that the new access to God, which is brought about by the heavenly journey and has as its goal the liturgical communion between God and Israel, cannot be an individual mystical experience. The Hekhalot literature does not propagate the *unio mystica,* the unification of the individual with God, but, if the expression is allowed, the *unio liturgica,* the liturgical communion of the *yored merkavah,* as emissary of Israel, with God.

Second, the aim of the adjuration is the command of the Torah and with it the command of the world through magic. If the heavenly journey is interwoven with magical elements, then the adjuration as the new form of the study of the Torah is nothing but pure magic. Everyone who knows the correct formulas of adjuration masters the Torah in a single act of illumination.

In the Hekhalot literature, the predominant magical moment is based on an automatism of cause and effect: the application of the correct formulas of adjuration causes the desired effect. Here, however, we are dealing with nothing less than a primitive hocus-pocus or abracadabra. The magical conception of the world in the Hekhalot literature is founded on the belief that all of reality consists of the names of God and the angels. At the same time, the names are the means and the goal of the adjuration. The knowledge of the divine name and its application in the magical adjuration are the keys to the understanding of the world. "God is his name" is the message; large sections of the Hekhalot literature can be read as a theology of the name, as an attempt to unfold the divine names. This explains the hybrid and often exhausting language of the Hekhalot literature, the endless lists of *nomina barbara,* and above all the *Shi*ʿ*ur Qomah*. We are not dealing with the mysterious meaning of something, the key to which we have unfortunately lost, nor with the enigmatic mathematical proportions of the divine appearance whose formulas we have not yet found; rather the "nonsense" is the message: everything consists of names. Whoever knows the names, knows the Torah and therefore the world as well.

One must even go a step further. God already becomes dependent on man through the heavenly journey, as the *yored merkavah*'s heavenly journey reveals that God, too, is dependent on the liturgical communion with Israel. This idea is not necessarily new: such a disposition is already present in rabbinic Judaism, for example in the dependency of God's kingdom on the liturgical acknowledgment by

Israel.[57] However, with man's theurgic power over God as expressed in the adjuration, a quality has been reached that far surpasses that which is possible in classical rabbinic literature. The *yored merkavah* who knows the names commands not only the Torah and the world, but finally God as well. By allowing the *yorede merkavah* to dismantle the borders between heaven and earth, God himself, in the end, has succumbed to their power. In a hardly surpassable manner, the "distant cosmocrator" has surrendered his fate to man.

[57]Cf. the *himlikhu* ("they installed you as king") together with Exodus 15:18 in the third benediction of the Shema' and Midrashim such as ShemR 23,1; see Schäfer, *Studien zur Geschichte und Theologie des rabbinischen Judentums*, pp. 30ff.; and M. Idel, *Kabbalah. New Perspectives*, New Haven and London, 1988, pp. 156ff.

Bibliography

Alexander, P. S. "The Historical Setting of the Hebrew Book of Enoch." *JJS* 28 (1977): 156–180.

———. "3 (Hebrew Apocalypse of) Enoch. A New Translation and Introduction." In J. H. Charlesworth (ed.), *The Old Testament and Pseudepigrapha,* Vol. 1. *Apocalyptic Literature and Testaments.* pp. 223–315. London, 1983.

———. "Comparing Merkavah Mysticism and Gnosticism. An Essay in Method." *JJS* 35 (1984): 1–18.

———. "Appendix: 3 Enoch." In E. Schürer, G. Vermes, F. Millar, and M. Goodman, *The History of the Jewish People in the Age of Jesus Christ,* vol. 3.1, pp. 269–277. Edinburgh, 1986.

———. "Incantations and Books of Magic." In E. Schürer et al., *The History of the Jewish People in the Age of Jesus Christ,* vol. 3.1, pp. 342–379. Edinburgh, 1986.

Altmann, A. "A Note on the Rabbinic Doctrine of Creation." *JJS* 7 (1956): 195–206.

Aptowitzer, V. "Zur Kosmologie der Agada. Licht als Urstoff." *MGWJ* 72 (1928): 363–370.

Bar-Ilan, M. *Sitre tefillah we-hekhalot.* Ramat-Gan, 1987.

Chernus, I. "Individual and Community in the Redaction of the Hekhalot Literature." *HUCA* 52 (1981): 253–274.

———. *Mysticism in Rabbinic Judaism.* Berlin and New York, 1982 [SJ 11].

Cohen, M. S., *The Shiʿur Qomah. Liturgy and Theurgy in Pre-Kabbalistic Jewish Mysticism.* Lanham, New York and London, 1983.

———. *The Shiʿur Qomah: Texts and Recensions*. Tübingen, 1985 [TSAJ 9].

Dan, J. "Hithawwuto u-megammotaw shel maʿaseh ʿasarah haruge malkhut." In E. Fleischer (ed.), *Studies in Literature Presented to Simon Halkin,* pp. 15–22. Jerusalem, 1973.

———. "Pirqe hekhalot u-maʿaseh ʿaseret haruge malkhut." *Eshel Beʾer Shevaʿ* 2 (1980): 63–80.

———. " ʿAnafiʾel, Meṭaṭron we-yoṣer bereshit." *Tarbiz* 52 (1982–83): 447–457.

———. "Three Types of Ancient Jewish Mysticism." Seventh Annual Rabbi Louis Feinberg Memorial Lecture in Judaic Studies, University of Cincinnati, 1984.

———. "Livʿayyat ha-periodizaṣiyah shel torat ha-sod haʿivrit mishilhe ha-ʿet ha-ʿatiqah el yeme-ha-benayyim," pp. 93–100. Proceedings of the Ninth World Congress of Jewish Studies, Division C, Jerusalem, 1986.

———. "Hekhalot genuzim." *Tarbiz* 56 (1987): 433–437.

———. (ed.). *Proceedings of the First International Conference on the History of Jewish Mysticism: Early Jewish Mysticism.* Jerusalem, 1987 [JSJT 6, 1–2].

Elbogen, I. *Der jüdische Gottesdienst in seiner geschichtlichen Entwicklung,* 3d ed. Frankfurt am Main, 1931; reprinted Hildesheim, 1967.

Elior, R. *Hekhalot Zuṭarti. Mahadurah madaʿit.* Jerusalem, 1982 [JSJT, Suppl. I].

Esh, S. *Der Heilige (Er sei gepriesen). Zur Geschichte einer nachbiblisch-hebräischen Gottesbezeichnung.* Leiden, 1957.

Even-Shemuel, Y. *Midresche Geʾullah, 2d ed. Jerusalem and Tel Aviv,* 1954.

Fishbane, M. *"The Holy One Sits and Roars": Mythopoesis and the Midrashic Imagination.* in print.

Geller, M. J. "Two Incantation Bowls Inscribed in Syriac and Aramaic." *BSOAS* 39 (1976): 422–427.

Goldberg, A. "Schöpfung und Geschichte. Der Midrasch von den Dingen, die vor der Welt erschaffen wurden." *Judaica* 24 (1968): 27–44.

———. *Untersuchungen über die Vorstellung von der Schekhinah in der frühen rabbinischen Literatur.* Berlin, 1969 [SJ 5].

———. "Einige Bemerkungen zu den Quellen und den redaktionellen Einheiten der Grossen Hekhalot." *FJB* 1 (1973): 1–49.

———."Der verkannte Gott. Prüfung und Scheitern der Adepten in der Merkavamystik." *ZRGG* 26 (1974): 17–29.

———. *Ich komme und wohne in deiner Mitte. Eine rabbinische Homilie zu Sacharja 2,14 (PesR 35)*. Frankfurt am Main, 1977 [FJS 3].

Goldschmidt, L. *Das Buch der Schöpfung*. Frankfurt am Main, 1894; reprinted Darmstadt, 1969.

Gordon, C. H. "Aramaic Magical Bowls in the Istanbul and Baghdad Museums." *Archiv Orietální* 6 (1934): 319–334.

———. "Aramaic and Mandaic Magical Bowls." *Archiv Orientální* 9 (1937): 84–106.

———."Two Magic Bowls in Teheran." *Orientalia* 20 (1951): 306–315.

Graetz, H. "Die Mystische Literatur in der gaonäischen Epoche." *MGWJ* 8 (1859): 67–78, 103–118, 140–153.

Grözinger, K. -E. *Ich bin der Herr, dein Gott! Eine rabbinische Homilie zum Ersten Gebot (PesR 20)*. Frankfurt am Main, 1976 [FJS 2].

———. "Die Namen Gottes und der himmlischen Mächte—Ihre Funktion und Bedeutung in der *Hekhalot*-Literatur." *FJB* 13 (1985):23–41.

Gruenwald, I. "Qeṭaʿim ḥadashim mi-sifrut ha-hekhalot." *Tarbiz* 38 (1968–69): 354–372; 39 (1969–70): 216–217.

———. "Qeṭaʿim ḥadashim mi-sifrut hakkarat-panim we-sidre-sirṭuṭin." *Tarbiz* 40 (1970–71): 301–319.

———. *Apocalyptic and Merkavah Mysticism*. Leiden and Cologne, 1980 [AGAJU 14].

———. "Shirat ha-malʾakhim, ha-qedushah u-veʿayyat ḥibburah shel sifrut ha-hekhalot." In A. Oppenheimer, U. Rappaport, and M. Stern (eds.), *Jerusalem in the Second Temple Period. Abraham Schalit Memorial Volume,* pp. 459–481. Jerusalem, 1980.

———. *From Apocalypticism to Gnosticism. Studies in Apocalypticism, Merkavah Mysticism and Gnosticism*. Frankfurt am Main, Bern, New York, and Paris, 1988 [BEATAJ 14].

———. (ed.). "Reʾuyyot Yeḥezqel." In *Temirin,* vol. 1, pp. 101–139. Jerusalem, 1972.

Halperin, D. J. *The Merkabah in Rabbinic Literature*. New Haven, Conn., 1980 [AOS 62].

———."A New Edition of the Hekhalot Literature." *JAOS* 104 (1984): 543–552.

———. "A Sexual Image in Hekhalot Rabbati and Its Implications." In J. Dan (ed.), *Proceedings of the First International Conference of the History of Jewish Mysticism: Early Jewish Mysticism,* pp. 117–132. Jerusalem, 1987 [JSJT 6, 1–2].

———. *The Faces of the Chariot. Early Jewish Responses to Ezekiel's Vision.* Tübingen, 1988 [TSAJ 16].

Herrmann, K. "Text und Fiktion. Zur Textüberlieferung des *Shiᶜur Qoma.*" *FJB* 16 (1988): 89–142.

——— and C. Rohrbacher-Sticker. "Magische Traditionen der New Yorker Hekhalot-Handschrift JTS 8128 im Kontext ihrer Gesamtredaktion." *FJB* 17 (1989): 101–149.

Hofius, O. *Der Vorhang vor dem Thron Gottes.* Tübingen, 1972 [WUNT 14].

Idel, *Kabbalah. New Perspectives.* New Haven, Conn., and London, 1988.

Isbell, C. D. *Corpus of Aramaic Incantation Bowls.* SBL Dissertation Series 17. Missoula, Mont., 1975.

Janowitz, N. *The Poetics of Ascent. Theories of Language in a Rabbinic Ascent Text.* Albany, N.Y., 1989.

Jellinek, A. *Bet ha-Midrasch,* vol. 5, 3d ed. Jerusalem, 1967.

Kadushin, M. "Introduction to Rabbinic Ethics." In *Jehezkel Kaufmann Jubilee Volume. Studies in Bible and Jewish Religion . . . on the Occasion of His Seventieth Birthday,* pp. 88–114. Jerusalem, 1960–61.

Kuhn, H. -W. *Enderwartung und gegenwärtiges Heil.* Göttingen, 1966 [STUNT 4].

Kuhn, P. *Gottes Trauer und Klage in der rabbinischen Überlieferung.* Leiden, 1978 [AGAJU 13].

Levine, E. *The Aramaic Version of Lamentations.* New York, 1976.

Levy, Y. *ᶜOlamot nifgashim.* Jerusalem, 1960.

Lewin, B. M. *Otzar ha-Geonim,* vol. 4/2 (Ḥagiga), Teil 1 (Teshuvot). Jerusalem, 1931.

Lichtenberger, H. *Studien zum Menschenbild in Texten der Qumrangemeinde.* Göttingen, 1980 [STUNT 15].

Lieberman, S. *Tosefta ki-fshutah,* vol. 4. New York, 1962.

———. "Metatron, the Meaning of His Name and His Functions." In I. Gruenwald, *Apocalyptic and Merkavah Mysticism,* pp. 235–241. Leiden and Cologne, 1980 [AGAJU 14].

Maier, J. "Das Gefährdungsmotiv bei der Himmelsreise in der jüdischen Apokalyptik und 'Gnosis'," *Kairos* 1 (1963): 18–40.

———. "Serienbildung und 'numinoser' Eindruckseffekt in den poetischen Stücken der Hekhalot-Literatur." *Semitics* 3 (1973): 36–66.

Marmorstein, A. *The Old Rabbinic Doctrine of God.* Oxford 1927–37.

McCullough, W. S. *Jewish and Mandean Incantation Texts in the Royal Ontario Museum.* Toronto, 1967.

Montgomery, J. A. *Aramaic Incantation Texts from Nippur.* Philadelphia, 1913.

Murmelstein, B. "Spuren altorientalischer Einflüsse im rabbinischen Schrifttum. Die Spinnerinnen des Schicksals." *ZAW* 81 (1969): 215–232.

Musajoff, S. *Merkavah Shelemah,* Jerusalem, 1921.

Naveh, J., and S. Shaked. *Amulets and Magic Bowls. Aramaic Incantations of Late Antiquity.* Leiden, 1985.

Odeberg, H. *3 Enoch or the Hebrew Book of Enoch.* Cambridge 1928; reprinted New York, 1973.

Reeg, G. *Die Geschichte von den Zehn Märtyrern. Synoptische Edition mit Übersetzung und Einleitung.* Tübingen, 1985 [TSAJ 10].

Reichman, R. "Die 'Wasser-Episode' in der Hekhalot-Literatur." *FJB* 17 (1989): 67–100.

Renner, L. "Qedusha und Hekhalot: Zum Verhältnis von synagogaler Liturgie und früher jüdischer Mystik." M.A. thesis, Berlin, 1989.

Schäfer, P. "Berēšīt bārā' Ĕlōhīm. Zur Interpretation von Genesis 1,1 in der rabbinischen Literatur." *JSJ* 2 (1971): 161–166.

———. *Die Vorstellung vom Heiligen Geist in der rabbinischen Literatur.* Munich, 1972 [STANT 28].

———. "Zur Geschichtsauffassung des rabbinischen Judentums." *JSJ* 6 (1975): 167–188. In idem, *Studien zur Geschichte und Theologie des rabbinischen Judentums,* pp. 23–44. Leiden, 1978 [AGAJU 15].

———. *Rivalität zwischen Engeln und Menschen. Untersuchungen zur rabbinischen Engelvorstellung.* Berlin and New York, 1975 [SJ 8].

———. "Der Götzendienst des Enosch." In idem, *Studien zur Geschichte und Theologie des rabbinischen Judentums,* pp. 134–152. Leiden, 1978 [AGAJU 15].

———. "Mahadurah biqortit shel Hekhalot Zuṭarti." *Tarbiz* 54 (1984): 153–157.

———. *Hekhalot-Studien*. Tübingen, 1988 [TSAJ 19].

———. "Ein neues Fragment zur Metoposkopie und Chiromantik." In idem, *Hekhalot-Studien,* pp. 84–95. Tübingen, 1988 [TSAJ 19].

———. "Jewish Magic Literature in Late Antiquity and Early Middle Ages." *JJS* 41 (1990): 75–91.

———. "The Ideal of Piety of the Ashkenazi Hasidim and Its Roots in Jewish Tradition." *Jewish History* 4 (1990): 9–23.

———. (ed.). *Synopse zur Hekhalot-Literatur.* Tübingen, 1981 [TSAJ 2].

———. (ed.). *Geniza-Fragmente zur Hekhalot-Literatur.* Tübingen, 1984 [TSAJ 6].

———. (ed.). *Konkordanz zur Hekhalot-Literatur,* vol. 1, Tübingen, 1986 [TSAJ 12]; vol. 2, Tübingen, 1988 [TSAJ, 13].

———. (ed.). *Übersetzung der Hekhalot-Literatur,* vol. 2. *Sections 81–334*. Tübingen, 1987 [TSAJ 17].

———. (ed.). *Übersetzung der Hekhalot-Literatur,* vol. 3. *Sections 335–597*. Tübingen, 1989 [TSAJ 22].

Schiffman, L. H., "A Forty-Two Letter Divine Name in the Aramaic Magic Bowls." *Bulletin of the Institute of Jewish Studies* 1 (1973): 97–102.

Schlüter, M. "Die Erzählung von der Rückholung des R. Neḥunya ben Haqana aus der *Merkava*-Schau in ihrem redaktionellen Rahmen." *FJB* 10 (1987): 65–109.

Scholem, G. "Hakkarat panim we-sidre sirṭuṭin." In *Sefer Assaf. Festschrift Simḥa Assaf,* pp. 459–495. Jerusalem, 1952–53.

———. *Major Trends in Jewish Mysticism, 3d ed.* New York, 1954; London, 1955 [1941]. *-Die jüdische Mystik in ihren Hauptströmungen*. Zürich, 1957; reprinted Frankfurt am Main, 1967.

———. "Tradition und Kommentar als religiöse Kategorien im Judentum." *Eranos-Jahrbuch* 31 (1962): 19–48.

———. *Ursprung und Anfänge der Kabbala*. Berlin, 1962 [SJ 3]. As *Origins of the Kabbalah*. Princeton, N.J., 1987.

———. *Jewish Gnosticism, Merkabah Mysticism, and Talmudic Tradition,* 2d ed. New York, 1965.

———. "Ein Fragment zur Physiognomik und Chiromantik aus der Tradition der spätantiken jüdischen Esoterik." In *Liber Amicorum. Studies in Honour of Professor Dr. C. J. Bleeker,* pp. 175–193. Leiden, 1969.

———. (ed.) "Havdalah de-Rabbi ʿAqiva." *Tarbiz* 50 (1980–81): 243–281.

Sjöberg, E. *Gott und die Sünder im palästinischen Judentum nach dem Zeugnis der Tannaiten und der apokryphisch-pseudepigraphischen Literatur.* Stuttgart, 1938 [BWANT 4, 27].

Swartz, M. D. "Liturgical Elements in Early Jewish Mysticism: A Literal Analysis of 'Maʿaseh Merkavah,'" Diss. New York University, 1986.

———. "*ʿAlay le-shabbeaḥ*—A Liturgical Prayer in *Maʿaśeh Merkabah,*" *JQR* 77 (1986–87): 179–190.

Uchelen, N. A. van. "Ethical Terminology in Heykhalot-Texts." In J. W. van Henten et al. (eds.), *Tradition and Re-interpretation in Jewish and Early Christian Literature. Essays in Honour of Jürgen C. H. Lebram,* pp. 250–258. Leiden, 1986.

Urbach, E. E. "Ha-masorot ʿal torat ha-sod bi-tequfat ha-tanna'im." In *Studies in Mysticism and Religion Presented to G. Scholem,* pp. 1–28. Jerusalem, 1967.

———. *The Sages. Their Concepts and Beliefs,* 2d ed. Jerusalem, 1979.

Wertheimer, S. A. *Batei Midrashot,* vol. 2, 2d ed. Jerusalem, 1954.

Wewers, G. A. "Die Überlegenheit des Mystikers. Zur Aussage der Gedulla-Hymnen in Hekhalot Rabbati 1,2-2,3," *JSJ* 17 (1986): 3–22.

Zunz, L. *Die gottesdienstlichen Vorträge der Juden historisch entwickelt.* Berlin 1832; 2d ed. Frankfurt am Main, 1892.

Index of Literature

Rabbinic Literature

Synopse zur Hekhalot-Literatur
(quotation according to sections)

Geniza-Fragmente zur Hekhalot-Literatur

Index of Authors

Index of Subjects

LaVergne, TN USA
10 March 2010
175506LV00001B/174/A

9 780791 410448